POWER
to
Reinvent Yourself

POWER
to
Reinvent Yourself

HOW TO BREAK THE DESTRUCTIVE
PATTERNS IN YOUR LIFE

<hr>

JASON FRENN

New York   Boston   Nashville

FaithWords
Hachette Book Group
237 Park Avenue
New York, NY 10017

www.faithwords.com

Printed in the United States of America

First Edition: October 2010

10 9 8 7 6 5 4 3 2 1

FaithWords is a division of Hachette Book Group, Inc.
The FaithWords name and logo are trademarks of Hachette Book
Group, Inc.

Library of Congress Cataloging-in-Publication Data

Frenn, Jason.
   Power to reinvent yourself : how to break the destructive patterns in your
life / Jason Frenn.—1st ed.
     p. cm.
   ISBN 978-0-446-54622-5
   1. Christian life.   2. Change (Psychology)—Religious aspects—
Christianity.   I. Title.
   BV4509.5.F7495 2010
   248.8'6—dc22
                    2009052851

To

A great person
A great Christian
A great example
A great mom

Roberta Hart

Contents

———— ∽∾ ————

Acknowledgments

———— ⌒∞⌒ ————

Thank You, God, for reaching into my heart and giving me life and freedom. All the truth, insight, and power found in the pages of this book come from You. Thank You for giving me such a great family (past, present, and future) and for helping us break the chains!

Thank you, Cindee, Celina, Chanel, and Jazmin (the ladies of my life) for encouraging, inspiring, and supporting me through this project. I am one of the most fortunate men on the planet, because you are some of the most wonderful people I know. I thank God for allowing me the privilege of having you in my life.

Thank you, Mom, for your wonderful support in

this project. I am very proud to be your son. You've become an outstanding example of what the power of God can do in the life of an individual, and that's why I am pleased to dedicate this book to you.

Thank you, Richard and Janice Larson, for being wonderful in-laws and for sharing two great stories with me that will greatly impact those who read this book.

Thank you, Dad and PJ, for always being there with a warm heart and an encouraging attitude. I am pleased to see the growth and maturity in your lives over the years. Thank you for loving me so faithfully.

Thank you, Steve Larson and Melodee Gruetz-macher, for taking the time to study this document and help me become a better writer. I love and appreciate you and consider myself a very fortunate brother-in-law to both of you.

Thank you, Kathleen Stevens, for poring over this book several times. You are a first-rate editor with a heart to help people understand truth and experience new beginnings. It was an honor to work with someone of your caliber.

Thank you, Holly Halverson, for being the principal editor and giving overall guidance on the project. God has given you a wonderful gift, and everyone who knows you feels the same! Thank you for stepping in when you did and helping me make this book what it has become.

Thank you, Joey Paul, for your friendship, wisdom, and spiritual concern for people. Hachette Book Group is a richer company because of your presence in the organization.

Thank you, Rolf Zettersten and Harry Helm, for inviting me to be a part of the FaithWords family. I am a very proud author to work with such a fine organization. Thank you, Shanon Stowe, Preston Cannon, Pamela Clements, and the entire sales force at Hachette Book Group. There are many people who dream of working with people as professional and as capable as you!

Thank you, Kristin Cole, Jodi Phillip, and A. Larry Ross, for helping us get the word out. Your friendship is something I cherish. I couldn't do it without you!

Thank you, Mari-Lee Ruddy, for always being a great friend and advisor. Thank you, Rick and Evangeline Zorehkey for being such great and inspirational examples to those who need God's power and love.

Do You Need the Power to Reinvent Yourself?

———— ⌒⧉⌒ ————

THE PHONE CALL CAME at one of the most difficult times in her life. Nearly three months after she watched her only son move with his wife and child to Costa Rica to be missionaries, her husband's physical condition had deteriorated considerably. In the span of a few short days, he lost his ability to speak. There was little hope for recovery. When the phone rang at 4:00 a.m., the voice on the other end somberly said, "I am sorry, Mrs. Hart. Your husband passed away this morning."

That day my mom, at age forty-six, became a widow. Her only companion was a small lapdog named Peanut. Over time, she sank into depression, and each day the walls seemed to close in a bit more.

After the death of her husband, my stepfather, Mom's alcohol use increased substantially. Every day at 5:00 p.m., she would pour herself the first of many drinks. By midnight, she would consume nearly fifty ounces of wine.

One night she reached the end of her rope and called me in Costa Rica from the United States. "My husband died and made me a widow," she said. "My grandchild no longer lives in this country. I see you every three or four years. I have no job. I have no friends. I have no family. I have no life!" Then there were no words, just sobs.

It was a painful moment. Anything I could have said had already been said. Any words of comfort would not have found a home in her heart. Even if they had, the alcohol would have erased them within minutes. It was only by the grace of God that Mom managed to get through the next several months. Given the fact that we lived over three thousand miles away, there were few options but to pray.

One afternoon, the middle-aged couple living next door invited Mom to join them for a few drinks and hors d'oeuvres. At first she was hesitant, because she was trying to cut back on her drinking. The neighbors were kind, though, and offers like that didn't come every day. So she agreed to go for a short visit. The conversation was light. The atmosphere was pleasant. It was perhaps the first time in months that she enjoyed herself.

After several hours, the festivities began to wind down. Mom graciously thanked her hosts and headed for the door. By then, it was dark. She took about five steps outside and realized that she couldn't see a thing. The absence of streetlights made the journey home challenging. The two glasses of wine didn't help either. Carefully placing one foot in front of the other, she continued the seventy-foot walk back to her house.

After she passed the property line and headed up the incline next to her porch, Mom's shoe caught the edge of a large stone. Before she knew what was happening, she fell face first into the large, jagged rocks that covered the embankment next to the driveway. Her nose was fractured. Her face was severely cut. Her head was spinning. With a minor concussion, she somehow stumbled onto the driveway, made it inside the house, and headed for the bathroom.

She took one look in the mirror, and the image staring back at her summed up what her life had become. She was a broken woman. In every sense of the word, she had hit rock bottom. With tears streaming down her face, mixed with trails of blood from her nose, my mother gingerly tried to clean her wounds. But it was too painful. She needed help. That's when she turned to a person who always seemed to lend a helping hand. She called a friend, who immediately came over.

As her friend began to clean the cuts on Mom's face, she said, "Tell me, Roberta. How did this happen?" My mom related the entire story. Her friend listened carefully and continued to touch up her cuts. When Mom concluded, her friend paused for a moment and asked if she could offer a simple piece of advice. "Sure," my mom said. Her friend then asked, "Why not give God a try? Why not come with me to a class where you can learn about God?"

Of all the possible questions her friend could have asked her, these were the most important. My mother's aha moment was fast approaching. The blinders she wore were beginning to come down, and she was able to see her life for what it truly was. Her relationships were full of conflict. She had not gained the upper hand over her drinking and was unable to correct her own destructive course. The physical damage to her face was a strong indication that she had to make a change and fast. This was a defining moment in her life. That night, she came to the most important realization of all: she needed to initiate a relationship with God.

The next morning, my mom—clean and sober— made the decision to call out to God and make Him Lord of her life. She prayed, "God, only You can help me turn my life around. You and I will have to make it happen." Over the next six months, she worked diligently to break the patterns of destruction and overcome everything that held her back.

Although my mom did not attend any alcohol recovery programs, she went to classes with her friend and began to read her Bible. Each day, she spent time in prayer and eventually attended church regularly. Her mind was renewed. Her spirit was rejuvenated. Her soul discovered hope. Her body recuperated from years of intoxication.

Months after her episode, my wife and I noticed a difference in my mom's demeanor. She was still pessimistic and, at times, very lonely. But God gave her the strength to stop drinking, and over the course of two years she became an entirely different person.

Today, she continues to practice the things that helped set her free. For the past several years, she has faithfully volunteered in many of our citywide crusades held in the United States. My mother has become an outstanding Christian and a caring human being.

It's been close to fifteen years since her severe bout with depression and alcoholism. What made the difference? She decided to partner with God, and together they formed godly and healthy habits that replaced the destructive ones. Today she is a woman of God, respected by friends and family. She is a great example of someone who was able to overcome the destructive patterns in her life.

Good people who come from good families are capable of making choices that derail their lives for decades. Other people come from dysfunctional homes where there is no apparent hope for breaking the cycle. Regardless of whether your background is healthy or dysfunctional, I believe you can access the power to reinvent yourself. This is what motivated me to write this book for you.

Is there something you want to change about your life? If so, what is it? Most people want to be happy, healthy, and financially stable. Are you all of these things? People also want to have decent friendships, peace of mind, and healthy family relationships. Do you have all of these things? You may be struggling with an addiction or suicidal thoughts that you can't seem to shake. As I write this book, I am convinced that God wants to give you the power to remove the destructive patterns in your life. He wants to help you live life in abundance (John 10:10). He wants to give you freedom, joy, peace, and the desires of your heart (Ps. 37:4). He wants to empower you to live a victorious life! So if you're not living the life you want, something needs to change.

CAN THIS BOOK CHANGE YOUR LIFE?

You may be wondering what this book offers that others don't. Of the millions of written works in the world, what makes this one unique and worth reading? Let me share why I believe you will benefit from reading this book.

Now more than ever people feel stuck, and they are sick of living in survival mode. Parents fear passing their baggage on to their children. Spouses don't want their marriages to end in a bitter divorce. People are tired of feeling helpless in the face of the addictions they can't seem to overcome. They don't want the pain of past hurts to keep them from moving forward. They don't want to sabotage their ability to move up the corporate ladder. We all want to break free from the things that hold us back.

In essence, all of us are looking for real power, the power that gives us victory over the things that have kept us in cycles of frustration and defeat. We all want to experience true freedom and peace of mind. We all want power to reinvent ourselves. What about you? Are you living the life you've always wanted or are you simply treading water? Are you looking for real power?

This book offers a godly approach to breaking the destructive patterns in our lives, especially those that are passed from one generation to the next. It focuses first and foremost on personal change through a partnership with God. It is filled with compelling biblical examples and powerful personal stories that demonstrate how God can transform any life—especially yours.

As a result of implementing the principles you learn in this book, you will experience victories in your personal life, marriage, family, and career. This book will equip you to walk in freedom from past hurts, something that comes with a real relationship with the living God. If you want to experience a significant breakthrough and enjoy the life you've dreamed of having, then this book is definitely worth reading. If you want to experience true freedom over the chains that have held you back, then this book can definitely change your life!

⚭

In the following chapters, you will learn six necessary steps that will help you live the life God wants for you and get past the things that hold you back. Chapter 1 explains that you first need to discover your reason for change—your *why*. Chapter 2 discusses how God can help you radically change your perceptions and so change your heart. Chapter 3 helps you identify the destructive patterns that keep you stuck in survival mode. In chapter 4, you will learn how to form godly habits that will inevitably help you make a quantum leap in many areas of your life. Chapter 5 will help you experience freedom from past hurts by learning to forgive and to receive forgiveness. Chapter 6 encourages you to establish a network of trusted friends so they can reinforce the work God has done in your life.

If you want to tap into the real power that only God can offer you, turn the page, and we'll begin the journey together.

CHAPTER 1

Discover Your Why

⸻ ❦ ⸻

HOW DOES CHANGE BEGIN? It doesn't start when we realize the mistakes we made and then try to correct them. Instead, the first step in breaking destructive patterns is to discover the reason we want to change. It's the reason that knocks us off our seats and causes us to move in a certain direction. This is known as the *why*.

As an international speaker I am constantly asked, "How can someone change?" In order for change to occur, the *how* is not nearly as important as the *why*. Whether you want to make money, lose weight, break an addiction, stop abusive behavior, ascend in your job, become the greatest in your field, or simply be a decent human being, discovering the reason why you want to change is the key. There are many books written on *how* to lose weight, become rich, be a better parent, raise godly children, and build a wonderful marriage. Regardless of the breakthrough you seek, only you can answer *why* you want to change. You will never attain what you want until you fully understand your *why*.

Why is your *why* so important? It's the reason for doing what you do. It's the motivation that drives you to move forward when you feel like staying the same. When you lack the energy to change, you will ultimately ask yourself, "Why should I do this?" If your answer is not convincing, then your *Yes, but…* will trump your why.

THE *YES, BUT*…

Is there an excuse you use to avoid doing what you should? Perhaps you've said, "I don't have enough time. I don't have enough money. I don't have the right contacts." Or maybe you've said, "I love food too much. I really enjoy shopping and can't resist a deal. I feel too overwhelmed and don't have the energy to contemplate change." This is what I call the *Yes, but*…. When your *Yes, but*…(your excuse) is bigger than your *why* (your reason for change), you will always feel frustrated. You will feel enslaved to the status quo and stuck in the patterns of destruction.

My mom could have allowed an excuse to keep her from the greatest decision of her life. But that didn't happen. Why? Because her *why* became more important than any excuse. She didn't allow an excuse to be larger than her motive to do what she needed to do.

Instead of letting excuses prevent you from moving forward, focus on an important reason for change. Then your *why* will be bigger than your *Yes, but…* and the foundation for change will be laid.

WHAT LEADS TO CHANGE?

As we begin our journey toward reinventing ourselves, we need to address one more important question: why do people change? The answer is simple. We change because staying the same becomes unacceptable. Generally, we alter our direction or behavior for one of four reasons. It's important to find the one that works for you—that drives you all the way through to the change you seek.

We Change Because We Are Afraid

The most common reason we change is *fear*. We're afraid of losing something. An impending doom—fear of death, losing our homes, losing friends, losing our jobs, losing our families, losing our spouses, or losing something of high value—hovers over our heads. Perhaps we fear physical, emotional, or financial punishment as a result of our current course of action.

Certain individuals change their ways only after bypass surgery or when faced with bankruptcy. Some people change because a spouse offers an ultimatum. Perhaps they change because their boss catches them doing something illegal, and they don't want to get fired. Over time, however, people can become desensitized to their fears, and as a result, they return to the same behavior that led them down the destructive path in the first place. So fear, although a powerful motivator, may not work for everyone.

We Change Because We Want to Reach a Goal

People also change because they set their hearts on something and will do anything to achieve it. Models lose weight. Investors raise money. Students sacrifice hours of sleep. Athletes train for years. Missionaries move halfway around the world, live in a foreign land, and learn a new language. But what happens when we reach the goal? What happens when we get what we want? The carrot dangling in front of our eyes must be constantly sweetened in order to entice us to move forward. More often than not, we move on to something new. Goal motivation can be a powerful motivator much like fear.

We Change Because We Are Disgusted

I find this reason humorous. I call it the *I'm thoroughly disgusted with* reason for change. We look through a forest of hanging clothes and say, "I have nothing to wear. Nothing fits." Then we mutter to ourselves, "There's no way I'm wearing sweats to church. I'd just as soon not go!" We're tired of not having anything in our bank account. We're sick of our hair, our glasses, our furniture, our job, our ignorance, or whatever else seems to irritate us.

Recently, I put on a few pounds. I wasn't happy about it, but at least I still had one pair of dress pants that fit. One morning I was heading to a jail to speak. I stopped into my favorite coffee shop and ordered my favorite drink. As I climbed into my truck and sat down, I heard a noise that sounded like a tear in the fabric of the driver seat. So I got out to inspect the damage. I didn't see anything. The seat looked intact. I did feel a draft on my backside, however. I turned around and saw a couple of people smirking at me from across the parking lot. When I looked over my shoulder and down my back, I discovered that I had split my pants from the belt all the way down to the beginning of the inseam. I wasn't about to show up and speak at a jail dressed like that. Needless to say, I found a reason to drop those pounds I had gained. Why? Because I was *thoroughly disgusted with* my weight.

While being *thoroughly disgusted with* is a powerful motivator for change, it may not work for everyone. After all, what happens when we reach our goal? How do we maintain our new status? The answer is we can't. No one can be disgusted with himself or herself and stay motivated for change for an extended period of time.

We Change Because We Want to Be Healthy

Another reason people change comes from the desire to grow and become healthy. In essence, it centers on a longing to mature and better ourselves. If our motive is good, we'll most likely move forward. If our reason is healthy and strong, the excuses we entertain will eventually dissipate. If our *why* is great, the *how to* will be easy to implement. Whether you are motivated by fears, goals, disgust, or a desire to simply grow and be healthy, know what puts fuel in your tank, what motivates you to change.

So dig deep, be honest, and ask yourself, "What's

the reason behind my desire to change? What's my why?" If you discover a strong enough reason for change, one that works for you, you'll have the necessary fuel to keep moving in the right direction. While it's true that we come to the point of wanting to change, God gives the power to do so.

My mom had a big why. She knew she needed to change, and she did so for good and right reasons. Because of that, she has grown and flourished in her relationship with Christ. The change in her life has had a profound impact on her family and friendships. All the areas of her life have been greatly enriched. It's a change that has lasted more than fifteen years.

How about your life? Do you have it all together? Is your life on target? Or are you stuck in the same patterns you've been stuck in for years? Are there issues in your life you've never been able to resolve? Do you need a breakthrough? Perhaps you're concerned about your marriage, kids, family, career, finances, health, or some other issue. If so, you probably need a helping hand, and I want to offer you that.

If you desire change, I've got good news for you, friend. God wants you to live a life of freedom, not oppression; of strength and courage, not fear and anxiety; of joy and satisfaction, not depression and discontent. Whether you come from a wonderful family with a rich heritage or from a dysfunctional home, God offers you the power to reinvent your life.

Without the power of God, breaking the cycle of sinful patterns is nearly impossible. But with God, *all things are possible* (Matt. 19:26).

CHAPTER 2

Change Your Perceptions

———— ⌒∞⌒ ————

SHE FOUGHT BACK the tears. Sitting with her knees pressed together in the dark, cold space, the six-year-old felt lonely and confused. Her siblings had disciplined her and locked her in a closet. She managed to catch her breath between the waves of sobs and peeked through a crack in the door to watch them work on their chores. Then, resting back on her heels, she continued to cry.

Finally, her older brother approached the crack in the door as if he knew the exact place from which she was observing them. Glaring into the crack he sternly said, "Margaret, we'll let you out, but only if you stop crying. If we hear more than a peep out of you, you'll be in there all night!"

Over time, she learned to protect herself from those

who hurt her by forming an emotional wall to shield the pain. Many times she felt herself saying, "I will never treat my husband and children like this!"

The family was in disarray due to the absence of healthy parents. Her father passed away when she was a little girl. Her mother was incapable of taking care of her because of deteriorating health. And as the youngest of twelve children, she watched half of her brothers and sisters die from childhood illnesses.

At age twenty-one, she was married and within two years had two children. Unfortunately, her husband was not supportive. In fact, he was neglectful. On several occasions, he hopped on his motorcycle and disappeared for weeks. Finally, just before deploying overseas, he called to tell her that he had filed for divorce. She was twenty-five.

Three years later, she married Robert, who was seven years younger. Her new husband was the opposite of his predecessor. He was industrious and highly responsible, but unfortunately, he had a demanding work schedule. He traveled for weeks at a time installing radar systems in airports across the United States. In addition, he spent an average of sixty hours a week at the office. His continual absences created a large void in the family, and with each passing year, Margaret and Robert grew apart.

As her older children moved away and her youngest daughter, Roberta, entered high school, once again Margaret felt lonely and abandoned. In spite of her good intentions, she found it difficult to break free from the abusive patterns she experienced as a child. She too became controlling and, at times, physically aggressive.

Conflict between Roberta and her mother escalated. Many times, Roberta came home from school to find her mother upset. Margaret would accuse her of doing things that she had not done. In a rage, Margaret would grab the nearest object and hurl it at Roberta in an explosion of anger. Roberta pulled away from her family, looking for ways to escape. Over time, she learned to protect herself from those who hurt her by forming an emotional wall to shield the pain. Many times she felt herself saying, "I will never treat my husband and children like this!"

After turning twenty, Roberta got a job as a hostess in a restaurant in the San Fernando Valley. It was there that she met Bob, a bartender. He enjoyed telling jokes and making his customers laugh. Roberta and Bob were married and later had a baby boy. That baby boy was me.

Three years after they married, though, their relationship fell apart. They decided to divorce. My father moved in with my grandmother, and my mom and I lived in the west end of the San Fernando Valley. My dad was a good father and tried to see me every day after school before he went to work at the bar. He loved me and he expressed that to me.

Until I was twelve, my mom spent many hours taking me to baseball practice and hockey games. She granted me freedoms and encouraged my development in lots of areas. All in all, she was a great mom who did a remarkable job raising me as a single parent.

Shortly after I turned twelve, we moved a hundred miles away to a small mountain community called Big Bear Lake. The move was a major turning point in my relationship with both my parents. Because of the distance between the San Fernando Valley and our new home, I saw my dad only a few hours every other Sunday. That was a loss I never anticipated. For the first six months, every time my father climbed into his car to return home from visiting me, I, a chubby little twelve-year-old, sat in the driveway with tears in my eyes, asking one question: "Why can't I see my dad more often?"

My mother had problems of her own. She couldn't find a job. She struggled to make new friends. She felt overwhelmed with loneliness. So in order to silence the haunting voices of anxiety, pain, and frustration, she turned to the one companion that millions of people around the world seek in their time of need. She drank every night.

Eight months after our arrival in the new town, Mom's old boyfriend unexpectedly drove up to the house in a brand-new sports car. *What an entrance!* I thought. I couldn't remember the last time she looked so excited to see someone. Voilà! Just like that, they started to date again. Within two years, they eloped to Reno, where she said yes to the five-times-divorced man who was thirty-two years older than she was.

Their dating years had been wild, but their marriage was explosive, much like trying to put out a fire with gasoline. In the mornings, he would complain about her drinking yet would be the first to serve up a cocktail in the afternoon. The craziness intensified because they spent time together only on the weekends. He lived and worked in Burbank, where his business was subject to the highly temperamental film industry, television networks, and NC-17 production companies.

Seeing all five of his ex-wives at family reunions made things interesting—and complicated. But despite his past, he was a good man and reached out to my mom as best as he could. Their marriage somehow survived many roller coaster dips with a few near derailments. As a fifteen-year-old, I sat on the sideline and watched Mom slip further into alcoholism and depression. It was a terrible chapter in my life, because I never felt that I could offer her any help.

In spite of her good intentions, Mom found it difficult to break free from the abusive patterns she experienced as a child. As in the generations that preceded us, the craziness repeated itself. Our home was filled with conflict and emotional abuse. Through it all, I never wondered why things were the way they were. It never dawned on me that she was caught in a pattern that was handed down from generation to generation. While many people in our family made a promise to break the cycle, they eventually discovered as parents that they too had slipped into the patterns of dysfunction.

Over time, I learned to protect myself from those who hurt me by forming an emotional wall to shield the pain. I distinctly remember one night standing in my room after a heated argument with my mom. When she stormed off, I said to myself, "When I grow up, I'm going to be different from my parents. I will never treat my wife and kids like this!"

In the midst of the confusion and pain, one day our neighbors living across the street invited me to church. The Sunday night I agreed to go, it was about twenty-eight degrees outside and lightly snowing.

My immediate family wasn't religious in any sense of the word. On occasion, my grandmother took me to her church, but most of the time the service was in Arabic. For the most part, I spent Sundays doing whatever came my way. My dad, who is in the Bartender Hall of Fame, would jokingly say, "If I ever walk into a church, the building will probably come crashing down." So I admit I felt a little uncomfortable about going to a religious event.

But I agreed to go with them. When we pulled into the parking lot, my apprehension was manifested by sweaty palms and a few butterflies in my stomach. My neighbors carried a Bible everywhere, which I felt was a bit weird. The one they had was huge, large enough to be considered a weapon. It must have weighed five pounds. Each page was uniquely decorated with different colored highlighted markings and personal notes.

To make matters more interesting, my neighbors were front-row believers. They rarely sat anywhere besides the front row. I would have felt more comfortable sitting in the parking lot fighting to stay alive in the freezing cold. As I walked down the center aisle, I thought, *Everyone knows I'm new. They'll probably be staring at me the whole night.*

No sooner had we sat down than a power failure affected the entire block the church was on. There we sat in total darkness. Within seconds, the words of my father came to mind. I seriously thought, *My dad must have been a prophet. My depravity has blown a transformer!*

Suddenly, the family's oldest son leaned over and sarcastically said, "You know, that has never happened in all the years I've attended this church until you walked in the door." I knew he was joking, but my self-esteem was as low as it could be.

The pastor asked the ushers to retrieve candles. Little did I know that those candles would come to represent God's illumination in my life.

There was enough candlelight for all 150 of us to feel comfortable when the service finally got under way. The pastor stepped behind the podium and talked about a God who loves and doesn't want to condemn. The message centered on a Christ who died for the sins of the world and how God had the power to transform any individual and give eternal life. He talked about a God who gives meaning and significance. He then asked a question that was to change my life: "Do you want to experience new life?"

I had never heard a message like that. Those words, like a cool rain falling over the desert, brought refreshment to my soul. I knew I wasn't perfect. No one had to tell me that I was not a part of a church or that things in my life were not good. While I sat in the church in the midst of my conflicted adolescent life,

God's love broke through, and that's when I suddenly had an epiphany.

Hold on a second! I thought. *God has the power to change anyone. And that anyone can be* me. I thought further, *God grants eternal life, and He chooses to grant me eternal life. If He can set the captive free, He can set me free too. He can break the patterns of destruction handed down from generation to generation. And He can start with me.*

In 1981 on that cold, wintry night, God began to change my life. He changed my heart, and in doing so, He changed my perceptions. By changing my perceptions, He changed who I was. That night, God broke the cycle of dysfunction that plagued my family for generations. I had a genuine change of heart. Within weeks, I started to read my Bible and regularly attend church with my neighbors. Although I continued to struggle in certain areas, partying with my high school friends became less attractive.

At first my parents thought I was going through a fad. Things at home didn't get better as a result of my finding Christ—they got worse. I had many disputes with my mom over my commitment to the Lord. After a few drinks, she would tell me that dedication to religion was useless. Or she would say, "You can pretend that things are different, but I know who you truly are." It seemed as if the more I went to church, read my Bible, and prayed, the greater the conflict we had. Although it was disheartening, deep down inside I knew it was the alcohol talking. I believed that one day the light of God would shine in her life.

Every day I asked God to intervene and rescue Mom from the alcoholism and dysfunction that kept her in chains. I wanted her to experience the same life-changing power that transformed me. I eventually discovered that indeed God answers prayer. The introduction of this book tells the powerful story of how her life was changed and how she lives a godly and fruitful life entirely devoted to the Lord. Friend, no prayer goes unheard. Over the years, I have discovered that God always has the last word!

My story is not uncommon. Millions of people around the world have a similar story. What about you? Did you promise to do things differently as an adult or never to treat your family the way you were treated? Do you struggle to break free from the things that hold you back? Are there things in your life that need to change? If so, I have good news for you. Change is possible. Real power can be yours. God grants that power to those who ask Him. How does change happen? Much like the story you just read, an important step in your powerful transformation is a change in perception.

A change in perception occurs when the scales that have blinded us fall from our eyes and we suddenly see clearly. It's that moment when the light goes on in our heads and we say, "Aha!" Most important, it's when we first recognize the need for God's involvement in our lives. If that never happens, we continue to live out a fantasy, barely survive dysfunctional relationships, or believe that life is as good as it's going to get.

No one is born with perfect perception. We all struggle to maintain a healthy mind-set. To make matters worse, Satan sets out to complicate the battle even more. The Bible says, "The god of this age has blinded the minds of unbelievers, so that they cannot see the light of the gospel of the glory of Christ, who is the image of God" (2 Cor. 4:4). Satan's task is to contort perception so that people are unable to see the truth. He blinds people so that they become unaware that their lives are a mess.

In contrast, God works to repair perception, and He initiates the process with an *aha* moment. His task is to give sight to the blind and allow them to see truth. We find wonderful examples of this throughout the ministry of Jesus. Of all His miracles recorded in the New Testament, He healed the blind more than any other afflicted persons. This has spiritual and psychological implications in addition to physical ones. God gives us the ability to see the error of our ways so that we can begin the process of changing our hearts.

When people say they've had a change of heart, they really mean they've had a change in the way they see things, a change in perception. They think differently than they did before. The way they viewed things and interpreted life has changed.

PERCEPTION VERSUS PERSPECTIVE

Perception shouldn't be confused with perspective. There is an important distinction between the two. I define *perspective* as a point from which we view something, figuratively or literally. It's the angle from which we see a house, building, sky, or some physical object. Or it might be the way we view something more abstract such as a personality, problem, or situation. I also define perspective as our placement in life. *Perception*, on the other hand, is much more subjective and internal. It's how we interpret the data entering our minds from any given *perspective*.

Imagine that you have the best seat in the stadium to watch the Super Bowl—a great perspective on the game. You are situated about twenty rows back so that you have a good perspective in relationship to height and depth to the field. You are seated in the shade so the sun is not blinding. Your seat is perfectly centered between both end zones. Then, as the game starts, you put on a blindfold. You can't see anything. You hear the roar of the crowd as one team approaches the other's goal line. What will your perception of the game be? Dark, confusing, and at times noisy! Although you were in a wonderful position and could potentially view the game from a great perspective, your perception of the game was heavily skewed.

In the same way, our perception either enhances or sabotages our ability to move past the things that hold us back. Education, wealth, and a good home can position us for a wonderful life, but unless our perception is healthy, the way we interpret life will be contorted. For that reason, there are those who are affluent, educated, and intelligent but who find it difficult to function to any normal degree. How many times have we turned on the news only to hear that another famous celebrity has been arrested on charges of DUI or domestic violence? How many times have we seen a music superstar or a comedian's young life snuffed out due to a drug overdose? Although these people supposedly had everything, their perception guided them to destruction.

On the other hand, many people have a healthy perception. They come from humble socioeconomic conditions and overcome impossible odds to become highly effective individuals, parents, and spouses. The difference wasn't where they were placed in life (their perspective), but how they viewed and interpreted life (their perception).

Unless your perception is healthy, it will lead you down a path of destruction. Regardless of the amount of money, fame, or connections you may have, without a godly mind-set—one that has been freed from the blinding of the enemy—you will always be a slave to the patterns of destruction. If you've never been able to get past the things that hold you back, you need a change of perception. You need a change of heart. The question is, can you change?

I believe that no matter how crazy your life may seem, change is possible. No addiction, dysfunction, destructive pattern, or craziness has to be permanent. Your future is not etched in stone. You were beautifully and wonderfully created in God's image, and He wants to give you a life full of freedom, peace, and significance. I believe He loves you and knows the great potential of your life. You have no greater ally, and that Ally is eager to bring change into your life.

RAGS TO RICHES TO RAGS TO RICHES

The first three chapters in Exodus give us an example of someone who underwent a radical change in perception. The king of Egypt felt intimidated by the growing strength and influence of the Israelites. In order to subdue their powerful expansion, he ordered his slave masters to oppress the Israelites. The slave masters forced them to build much of the nation's infrastructure. Over the years, the Egyptians worked them ruthlessly.

Then Pharaoh called the midwives together and told them to kill every Hebrew baby boy whenever they assisted in a delivery. When the midwives refused, Pharaoh grew angry and issued the most serious decree in the history of his nation: *throw every firstborn Israelite into the Nile River.*

When a certain woman from the Israelite tribe of Levi gave birth to a son, she feared for his life. She managed to keep him hidden for three months. When she could no longer keep his life a secret, she placed him in a basket and took him to the edge of the Nile, wedging his floating crib in among the reeds.

That day, Pharaoh's daughter was bathing in the river and saw something peculiar along the bank. After sending her slave girl to retrieve the basket, she looked inside. She discovered a three-month-old baby who was crying his heart out. Feeling sorry for him, she decided to adopt him. She gave him the name Moses.

Although he was born into a poor home, he spent

his adolescent years in the palace. He went from rags to riches. One day, Moses saw an Egyptian punishing an Israelite and welled up with anger. He struck the Egyptian and killed him. When the king heard what Moses did, he tried to have him killed. Moses fled into the desert and once again found himself living in poverty. He had no family. He had no friends. He had no contacts. He lost everything and had to start all over again.

While Moses was in exile, Rameses became the new Pharaoh. He inherited incalculable riches, tens of thousands of soldiers, and over a million slave laborers to build cities and monuments. Rameses had everything a leader could want. He had one of the best perspectives available to human beings. As he stepped into the most powerful position on the planet, he oppressed the Israelites more than any previous king.

Moses, on the other hand, was in a different place in life. He had gone from rags to riches and back to rags. I am sure he thought about the things he had lost—living in the palace, the enormous wealth, the prestige of being the adopted grandson of a pharaoh. He probably second-guessed a time or two his decision to kill and run.

I'm not sure whether he felt depressed or lonely. But I am certain of one thing: Moses needed God's help to rebuild his life. He needed a complete paradigm shift.

Little did he know that God was going to give his perception a complete overhaul.

A few years later, Moses was tending a flock belonging to his father-in-law, Jethro. He led the sheep near a mountain called Horeb. From a distance, he saw a bush that was on fire but did not burn up. He began climbing the mountain, trying to get a closer look. Suddenly he heard a voice coming from within the bush: "Do not come any closer," God said. "Take off your sandals, for the place where you are standing is holy ground" (Exod. 3:5).

Moses froze.

Realizing Moses was taken aback by the strange phenomena, the Lord said, "I am the God of your father, the God of Abraham, the God of Isaac and the God of Jacob" (v. 6), meaning He was the same God worshiped by Moses' ancestors. At that, Moses hid his face because he did not want to look at God.

The Lord continued, "I have indeed seen the misery of my people in Egypt. I have heard them crying out because of their slave drivers, and I am concerned about their suffering. So I have come down to rescue them from the hand of the Egyptians and to bring them up out of that land into a good and spacious land, a land flowing with milk and honey" (v. 8). Then the Lord said something that Moses never anticipated: "I am sending you to Pharaoh to bring my people...out of Egypt" (v. 10).

Wait a minute! Moses thought. *I can barely lead myself, let alone a nation.* This wasn't just a simple career change God suggested. It required a total perception transformation.

Mustering up courage, Moses responded timidly to God's directive. "Who am I, that I should...bring the Israelites out of Egypt?" (v. 11).

God's answer was succinct yet powerful: "I will be with you" (v. 12).

To complete the mission, Moses didn't need political contacts. He didn't need an army. He didn't need money. He needed one thing: God's presence. Whatever the challenge, God's presence would make it manageable. In fact, God's biggest obstacle wasn't Pharaoh. It wasn't freeing the slaves. It was changing Moses' perception and convincing him that he was the right person for the job.

Moses had another question. When the people asked Moses who sent him, what was he supposed to tell them? God's answer was authoritative. It was a description of the creator of the universe not bound by time or space: tell them "I AM has sent me to you" (v. 14). The words were thunderous and the encounter was sufficient to change the mind-set that kept Moses bound for years. At that moment on a mountain, the Almighty had spoken. His words were clear, and Moses understood that God was with him. He realized that God was bigger than his circumstances. He had a radical encounter that produced a radical transformation in his perception. He had a change of heart. As a result, he came off the mountain a transformed man.

Moses returned to Egypt and led his nation out of the oppressive hands of the Egyptians. He did so with the vengeance of ten unparalleled plagues that left their mark in the history books. He defeated Rameses as God demonstrated His omnipotent power.

Moses was born into a humble home. The perspective from which he started his life was one of poverty and slavery. At approximately forty years of age, he lost everything he had gained and fled for his life into the desert. But with God, he overcame insurmountable odds and became one of the greatest leaders in history. He had gone from rags to riches to rags to riches.

Pharaoh, on the other hand, is mentioned only within the pages of Egyptian history and the context of his own dynasty. Rameses was born in the palace. He had wealth, contacts, and power. He had glory and even a godlike status. His position was great. His perspective was great. But compared to Moses, he had little impact upon the world.

What was the difference between Moses and Rameses? Moses had an encounter with the living God. The encounter was so dynamic that it transformed him from head to toe. He went up the side of a mountain as a migrant shepherd and came down with a holy mandate to become the leader of a nation. Through that encounter, God took a poor man, someone who gained much and lost it all, and transformed him into one of the most influential people the world has ever seen. Moses realized he needed to change, and he yielded to the One who had the capacity to change him.

WHAT ABOUT YOU?

If you desire to live life and not simply survive it, acknowledge your need for change. Half the battle is seeing who you are, including all your problems. Why is this so important? Change is impossible for those who don't believe they need help.

Removing the blindfold allows you to see your life for what it truly is. Once you are willing to recognize that certain things are not right, you can then yield to the One who has the capacity to change you. So take a good look in the mirror and ask yourself, "Am I getting past the things that hold me back? Or am I stuck in a destructive pattern?"

Perhaps you feel as though you are floundering through life. Maybe you've lost much, and you are disappointed with the person you see in the mirror. You might be wondering if anything you do really matters. Have you ever said, "When I grow up, I'm going to do things *differently*! I'm going to be *different*!" But you've discovered that you are repeating the same dysfunctional patterns you witnessed while growing up. If you see the need for change, congratulations! You are in a wonderful place to begin the process of transformation. Let me tell you why.

Change starts when we open our hearts and ask for help. Once we come to a place where we say, "God, I need your help to change," He can begin the process of rebuilding our lives. God wants to help you overcome destructive patterns. He wants to help you get past the things that hold you back. But His work begins only when you give Him permission. Admitting you don't have it all together is a major step in the right direction. If you have come to the place where you're ready to say, "God, I need Your help to change," He will give you the power to reinvent yourself.

TOTAL TRANSFORMATION

The people we've talked about in the first chapters illustrate that a radical change of heart begins with an encounter with God. It comes when we understand that God has a better plan than ours. It comes when we decide to change our perspective and yield to the One who has the capacity to change us.

It's important to note that just because we've discovered the need for change doesn't mean that we are changed. Many people know what they need to do but do nothing. In order for change to come, God must have full access to our hearts and our minds.

⌛

A young girl named Annie ran onto our crusade site in a panic. Looking over her shoulder like someone fleeing a predator, she pushed her way through the crowd of five thousand people to the base of the stage. The tears on her face were not tears of joy.

One of the ushers intercepted her before she launched up the stairs. Holding her, she bent down and asked, "What seems to be the matter?" The little girl turned to the forty-year-old crusade worker and whispered several sentences into her ear. The usher slowly moved her hand and covered her own mouth.

When she raised her head to make eye contact with me, the look in her eyes depicted horrific news.

Before I tell you more of Annie's story, you need to meet Stanley. Several years before that night, we had held a citywide crusade in the same area. The weather was beautiful, and the attendance was an all-time high for us. Thousands of people had traveled many miles to attend the three-day event. Each night, the momentum built until finally we had the biggest crowd the city had ever seen.

A young man entered the event from the farthest entrance. When he reached the outer perimeter of the crowd, he stood for a few moments and listened to the tail end of the message. His name was Stanley. The 6'2" twenty-year-old had a dark complexion and a muscular build. His half-buttoned shirt revealed a gaudy gold chain resting upon his hairless chest. His intimidating stature, though, was matched by his daunting reputation.

Stanley was involved in a gang in the city. Everything from auto theft to drug trafficking flowed under his supervision. Apparently two of the members had decided to leave the gang as a result of attending the crusade the night before. So he came to threaten us and stop the attrition.

I concluded the twenty-five-minute message with one simple question: "Do you want to experience true freedom?" Then I gave the crowd the opportunity to come to the stage for prayer. Several hundred people walked forward to find the freedom that only God can give from the destructive patterns in their lives.

There was something about the question that rattled this criminal to the core. For several minutes Stanley stood at the back of the large field staring at the stage and contemplating his life. Initially, the question irritated him. *I am free! I do whatever I want, whenever I want!* he thought. Perhaps what truly bothered him was the underlying question, "Are you *truly* free?"

For years Stanley had tried to build wealth and find real power. He made money and was one of the most powerful leaders in the city. But the one thing he searched for his entire life had evaded him.

He began to ask himself, *Am I truly free? How many lives have been destroyed in my quest for freedom?* In a matter of seconds, the blindfold fell from his eyes, and he could see his life for what it truly was.

Almost in slow motion, Stanley raised his hand and began to walk forward to the base of the stage. Something miraculous was taking place in his heart. His perception was being transformed. By the time he reached the platform, an isolated tear rolled down his left cheek. He lifted his eyes to heaven and said, "God, I need your help to change." That night, he asked the Lord to forgive him and committed his life to a real relationship with God.

Change began immediately. Stanley's transformation was radical. He left the gang and began to recruit members to work with him in a local church he started to attend. Gang activities in that city dropped to an all-time low and he eventually became a worker in his local church.

⌒∞⌒

As I stood on the edge of the platform two years later, the usher signaled me to speak to the little girl. I walked down the stairs located in the center of the stage and joined the two of them. Annie was sobbing. Her left arm was wrapped around her stomach. Her right hand was covering her nose and mouth. I gently placed my hand on her shoulder and said, "What's wrong, sweetheart?"

All the years of ministry never prepared me for what I was about to hear.

She managed to catch her breath and said, "My mother's boyfriend has been raping me for years. He said that if I ever told my mother, he was going to kill me."

I did my best not to look shocked.

Annie continued, "This morning, I woke up, and I

couldn't take it anymore. So I told my mommy every-thing. Then she threw him out of the house. When I walked outside this afternoon, he was waiting for me on the street corner. I ran as fast as I could, and he chased me to this soccer field. That's him standing over there."

When I looked up, I saw a grown man leaning against the archway of the only exit.

A plethora of emotions began to run through me. For the first time I could remember, I was speechless.

I knew that regardless of what I did, the evil man would always be lurking around. The power was out of my hands. The first solution that popped into my head wouldn't have been prudent, especially for a minister.

Yes, I could contact the authorities, but I felt the young lady was in immediate danger. She needed an immediate solution, but I struggled to find one. Then I remembered the correct starting point for any dilemma. I prayed.

After about ten seconds, I looked up. The man was still waiting at the exit, but someone else was walking toward us. His stature was unmistakable. He was tall, muscular, and full of energy. He happened to be one of the coordinators in charge of plugging people into small groups after the crusade. It was Stanley.

He asked, "Why such a long face?" I explained everything the young girl had told us. He slowly leaned back, took a deep breath, and exhaled. He asked, "Where's the guy?"

I wasn't sure if his question was unassuming or if there was an underlying motive. I pointed to the exit where the man was standing. Stanley looked the man over momentarily and turned back to me and confidently said, "I'll take care of it." At that moment, I didn't know what to think of his comment. I never felt that Stanley would act violently toward the man, and I wasn't in a position to accompany him to the exit. We were still in the midst of the service. So I watched from the stage.

Stanley calmly made his way to the exit. When the man saw him approaching, he lowered his head much like a disobedient dog that has been confronted by his master. Because of the hundred yards that separated us, it was difficult to determine what was said. Stanley spoke briefly and pointed at the man's chest only once. Then Stanley motioned toward the exit. The man turned and left.

I have no idea what Stanley said. I couldn't tell you if he told the man to leave and never return or if he told him about God's love. Two things are certain. Years after that incident, Stanley told me that he never heard about the man returning to that neighborhood to confront the young girl again. And, to this day, Stanley is still serving in ministry. The point is simply this: God took someone who led a life of delinquency and violence and transformed him into someone who could bring help to the hopeless.

Much like Moses, Stanley had a dynamic encounter with the living God at a time when he least expected it. Only God could bring about such a breathtaking change in his perception and in his heart. Once his transformation was under way, he was able to help others in his community.

This second step to moving past the things that hold you back—changing your perceptions—involves seeing who you are, including all your problems, and partnering with God to initiate the change. This means that the scales on your eyes must fall so you can see your life for what it is. It's more than just an aha moment. It means that you turn to God for help and develop a personal relationship with Him.

As you seek to change your perception, your relationship with God is crucial, because He reflects back to you the true condition of your character, disposition, and attitude. One important tool you can use to develop a new perception is the Bible. It acts as God's mirror for your life, and when you embrace it, you begin to see clearly. Another important help God offers are those who have a genuine desire to help you discover truth. If you reach out to those who are godly and wise, they will give you a clear picture of who you truly are. I will talk more about the role that godly people play in our lives in chapter 6.

Perhaps you come from a family where dysfunction has left its mark on several generations. Maybe you have said on more than one occasion, "When I grow up, I'm going to be different from my parents!" Or you might have been raised in the church, but you struggle to move past the things that hold you back. Whether your story is like Stanley's, mine, or someone else's, God wants you to experience a powerful transformation. According to Him, you are the apple of His eye (Zech. 2:8). He is with you and will never abandon you.

If you've never gained victory over the issues that seem to keep you in a never-ending cycle of frustration, God wants to give you a new perception that will bring about the breakthrough you seek. He offers you a helping hand at this crossroad and at this moment. How does such a wonderful change start? It begins with a personal relationship with Him.

⚭

As we close this chapter, let me ask you one final question. Do you want to experience true freedom? If so, there is something important we can do together.

We must wipe the slate clean and begin that real relationship with God. True freedom can only come as a result of a real connection with God. This is the essence of a change of perception and of heart.

Right now, I encourage you to look for a place where you can be alone with God. Then take a few moments to talk with Him. If you need a guide, I have included a simple prayer that will help you get started:

Lord, I am not quite sure how I arrived here or exactly where I am going, but one thing is certain: I need Your help to change my perception. I need You to change my heart. Help me to see things the way You see them. I recognize that I cannot change my life alone. I am sorry for all the damage I have done to those around me. Forgive me for all my offenses. I commit myself to a relationship with You and embark upon an adventure of getting to know You. Most importantly, I commit myself to whatever You ask of me during this process of change. Help me to be strong, obedient, and open to Your change for my life. Make Yourself real to me with each passing day. I pray these things in Christ's name. Amen.

CHAPTER 3

Break the Cycle of Destructive Behavior

———— ⌗ ————

A S JESSICA CAME DOWN the stairs, her mother took one look at her and said, "You're not leaving the house dressed like that!"

"What do you mean?" Jessica responded, pretending to be shocked.

"Do you really need me to say it again?" Shelly replied. "Your skirt is too short."

The sixteen-year-old's reaction was a poor attempt at looking confused. "I don't understand."

Shelly paused for a moment and slowly reiterated, "What part of 'too short' don't you get?"

"But Mom—" Jessica started to protest.

"Don't 'but Mom' me. Get back in that room and

put something decent on. I really don't want to tell you again."

Rolling her eyes, Jessica stomped up the stairs and thought, *Fine. Whatever. I can't wait until I turn eighteen so I can get out from under this totalitarian regime.*

When Jessica had changed clothes, she and her mom got into the car and headed to school. Shelly turned down the radio to ask her daughter, "Did you finish all your homework?"

"Yes, Mother."

"What's with your tone? Listen, your dad and I are a little concerned."

"What is it now?"

Taking a deep breath, her mother continued, "We noticed that you no longer want to spend time with your friends at church. As a matter of fact, you've opted out of going to youth group for about three weeks now. And you seem to be spending money like it's going out of style. For the life of us, we can't figure out how you go through so much cash."

"Yeah, well, the kids at church are boring," Jessica replied, managing to skirt the financial inquiry. "The boys sit around and play video games, and the girls huddle together in their stupid little cliques and discuss which boys are cute. I'd rather be with my real friends at the mall than go to church."

Shelly's heart sank. That was not what she wanted to hear her daughter say.

"Well, honey, we don't go to church because of the cool people who hang out there. We go because we want to develop our relationship with God."

"Mom, do you have any idea what people do when they are not at church? And then they show up and pretend to be holier than thou. At least my friends at school are consistent."

"Well, Jessica, I've heard that some of those friends of yours are into parties and inappropriate behavior."

"Oh, Mom, don't believe everything you hear. You always say that we shouldn't be gossipers."

"Honey, I'm just concerned. That's all."

As Jessica stared out the window, she felt confident that she had concealed her occasional dabble with the amphetamine Ecstasy. "Don't worry about me, Mom. I'll be just fine."

Deep down inside, Shelly knew that Jessica wouldn't be fine. Her motherly instincts were spot on. She tried to resist displaying the pain in her heart. At least the sunglasses covered her eyes, which welled up with tears.

When they pulled into the school parking lot, four

of Jessica's friends stood along the curb. Jessica enthusiastically greeted her entourage. The car door closed, and Shelly continued on her way. *Where did we go wrong?* she asked herself.

Within a minute, Jessica forgot about her mother's comments and focused her attention on what was important to her: friends, boys, and cheerleading.

Later, after graduating high school, Jessica went to junior college for a year. By twenty-five, she was married with a second child on the way. By age thirty-five, she was divorced, engaged to her live-in boyfriend, and shared custody of the two boys with her first husband.

The pressures of life were overwhelming for Jessica. Her occasional drug use in high school had developed into a consistent drinking habit. In order to cope, each night she poured herself several glasses of a distilled spirit. She felt lonely and reached out to a liquid companion that never rejected her. Like most who struggle with alcoholism, she never thought her problem was out of control. As long as her drinking didn't affect anyone else, she felt that it was a private matter, not a moral one.

One night Jessica poured herself a nightcap. She held up the glass to examine the interaction between the ice and gin. That's when she caught her reflection in the mirror. A most unsettling feeling came over her. The resemblance was astonishing. She had become the very person her mother feared she would become.

JOANNA'S STORY

Brian, frustrated when neither his wife nor his teen-aged daughter was ready to walk out the door, called out to fifteen-year-old Joanna, "Can we leave *today*?" After three minutes, he pulled out his phone and began surfing the Web.

Not two minutes had passed when he screamed at the top of his lungs, "Crystal, why can't you ever be ready on time?" An unintelligible rebuttal came from the master bathroom upstairs. One thing was certain, his wife didn't sound happy.

Brian was a morning person, always up by 5:30 a.m. He was industrious and worked over sixty hours a week. Aside from a short temper and perfectionist personality, he did his best to provide for the three-member household and their 3,500-square-foot upper-middle-class home. The one habit that stood out, though, was his addiction to the Internet. Many times he would bury himself in his home office and navigate for hours.

Finally, Crystal came downstairs. "Where's Joanna?" Brian asked.

"She's not ready yet. And that's a good thing, because I want you to explain this," Crystal said, throwing the credit card statement at him. "I discovered it this morning in your to-be-filed basket." He bent down to pick it up. A $483 charge was circled in blue marker.

"What?" he mumbled.

"Is that Internet porn?" Crystal asked.

He paused for a moment. Before he could squeak out a response, she shouted, "Don't lie to me! I can make a phone call right now and find out!"

"I can explain."

"I can't believe it," she said. "How long has this been going on?"

"Not very long."

"This is the third time I've seen a charge on our statement for over four hundred dollars. Is there someone else?"

"No, of course not."

"How can I be sure? You've lied about this sort of thing before," she tearfully replied.

"There's no one else. I promise."

Brian never thought his problem was out of control. As long as it was something that no one else knew about, he felt that it was not a moral matter, but a private one. Besides, he thought, Crystal had become rather cold over the years. The frequency of their intimacy went from several times a week to several times a month to several times a quarter. Occasionally he would give her flowers and take her out for dinner and a movie, but the icicles in their romance never melted. Because of his loneliness, he reached out to a virtual companion that never rejected him.

"My mom warned me about the things that are handed down from one generation to the next. Your father was a womanizer, and I've married a man who has become his father. You're just like him," Crystal said.

"Oh yeah? Well it seems as though I've married a woman who became her mother. It's no wonder your dad cheated on her all those years! She never displayed any affection toward him. He may as well have been married to a mannequin."

Crystal gritted her teeth. "I can't believe you. You're some piece of work."

Brian continued, "I've got needs too, you know. You think I enjoy my life? You think I like getting my needs met through an imaginary rendezvous with someone who lives in cyberspace?"

Finally, their daughter came into the kitchen. An awkward moment of silence ensued.

"Uh, are you guys ready?" Joanna asked.

"Yeah, we're ready," Brian said somberly.

"I'm not going." Crystal burst into tears.

Brian just looked at the floor.

"What? What do you mean?" Joanna asked.

"Both of you, just go!" Crystal cried.

Joanna was completely confused, although it wasn't the first time she had seen her mother in tears from a heated dispute with her dad. For the past six years, she watched her parents grow apart. Each fight seemed to drive a wedge that separated them more and more. Rarely did she see them smile or hold hands. Joanna knew one thing—she did not want to repeat the same patterns of destruction she saw in her parents' marriage. She wanted to break the cycle and someday have a healthy family filled with love and appreciation. More than anything she wanted to stop the hypocrisy that was so obvious, even to a fifteen-year-old.

"Come on, Crystal," Brian said. "Let's deal with it this afternoon. Besides, you'll be late for rehearsal."

Crystal knew her husband was right. It was her duty to pull herself together and be a good wife and mother. Asking for a minute to touch up her makeup and regain her composure, she headed to the guest bathroom with her purse.

On the way to the rehearsal, Brian obeyed the speed

limit and didn't roll through any stop signs. Hardly a word was spoken during the seven-minute drive.

The family managed to change their demeanor just as they pulled into the parking lot. Although on the outside the family looked normal, internally the conflict was still simmering. They joined several hundred people who walked into church that Sunday morning. Crystal headed to the choir room to begin rehearsing for her solo.

Over the years, Joanna continued attending church in spite of the family dysfunction. At times, she went alone and got a ride from a friend in the youth group. Eventually her parents divorced and went to different churches. During her years in college, she attended a small-group Bible study.

One night, she made a pact with God. She decided that in order to tap into the power necessary to break away from the past and move beyond the things that held her back, she would need to engage in a real relationship with God. Being religious wasn't enough. Church attendance wasn't enough. Being good wasn't enough. Joanna discovered that only a real relationship with the living God grants people the power to experience true freedom. That night changed her life forever.

After college Joanna married a Christian man, and

they had three lovely children. Although the first ten years were challenging, they managed to establish a healthy marriage and develop healthy family relationships. Until this day, however, she carries a faint concern that their relationship might end up just like her parents'. It serves as the motivation to keep her moving in the right direction.

Both of these stories illustrate a simple truth. If you leave generational dysfunction unattended, it will inevitably repeat itself. Regardless of your background, there are no guarantees for a smooth, trouble-free life. Whether your family is devout or has no spiritual sense whatsoever, you alone determine your spiritual health. Jessica followed her own desires and ended up starting patterns of dysfunction. In contrast, Joanna reinvented herself by being aware of what held her back and asking God to change it.

In the previous chapter, we asked God to change our perceptions and help us see our lives for what they truly are. The scales dropped from our eyes, and the aha moment gave us an opportunity to take the most important step in the process for change. We initiated a relationship with God.

In this chapter, we will learn how Christ can help us move beyond the destructive patterns previous generations in our families embraced. And, we will discover several keys to breaking those destructive cycles. These keys will help us experience true freedom and positively affect the precious generations that follow us.

YOU DON'T HAVE TO
BECOME YOUR MOTHER

At one time or another, many women mutter under their breath, "I don't want to become my mother." Men feel the same way about their fathers. Whether we love or despise our parents, there seems to be a common thread woven throughout the human heart. We prefer to be different from those who raised us.

The way they walk, talk, react, think, even the ways they reared us are things we want to do differently when we become adults. As we discover that many of our parents' tendencies are natural to us, we feel uneasy. It's even worse when someone speaks those dreaded words: "You're just like your mother!" "You're just like your father!" Although we want to be free to be our own person, we struggle to break the cycle.

In the book of Exodus we find an interesting insight on how sinful patterns are passed from parents to children. When God handed Moses two stone tablets that contained the Ten Commandments, He told him there were serious repercussions for those who break the rules (Deut. 28:15–68). God gave the Law for everyone's benefit and protection. But if we break certain commandments, the consequences impact not only us but our family and the generations that follow.

The Ten Commandments serve as a basis for moral living and ethical conduct in most countries around the world. A vast majority of all judicial systems embrace at least half of the commandments as their starting point for the rule of law.

The first two commandments deal with idolatry and lay out the consequences for those who break them.

The Israelites had left Egypt and begun the trek to the land God promised they would claim as their own. They traveled across the Red Sea and headed into the desert. Exodus 20 begins with God establishing His right and authority to give the commandments: "And God spoke all these words: 'I am the LORD your God, who brought you out of Egypt, out of the land of slavery'" (Exod. 20:1).

In essence He said, *I demonstrated my power over Pharaoh. I pulled you out of slavery. I sent the plagues upon Egypt. I performed miracles, signs, and wonders. I delivered you from the most powerful tyrant in the world. Therefore, I have the authority to give the following commandments. Now, then, this is what I want from you....*

Then we see the first two commandments as He gave them to Moses: "You shall have no other gods before me. You shall not make for yourself an idol in the form of anything in heaven above or on the earth beneath or in the waters below" (Exod. 20:3–5).

To the Lord, idol worship is a serious offense. If we worship anyone or anything but God, we reject His lordship. The Bible likens it to spiritual adultery (Hosea 1:2), and the consequences for such a practice are severe. For that reason two commandments out of the ten are dedicated to this theme, and six verses deal with those first two commandments. Furthermore, God dedicates an entire verse to explaining the punishment for breaking the first two commandments: "You shall not bow down to them or worship them; for I, the LORD your God, am a jealous God, punishing the children for the sin of the fathers to the third and fourth generation of those who hate me" (Exod. 20:5).

Like most, I struggle with the concept of a God who punishes children for the sins of their parents. How could God—who claims to be just—punish innocent children for the mistakes of past generations?

God does not lead us into temptation (James 1:13). He doesn't teach us to sin, worship idols, or break His laws (Lev. 25:18). He also doesn't single out children for the purposes of destroying their lives (Mark 10:13; Exod. 22:22). That is not His nature! He simply corrects those who break His commandments. I should not ask, *How could God punish children for their forebears' sins?* but *Who is responsible for teaching children to break God's laws?*

If God doesn't lead people into the destructive patterns that are passed from one generation to the next, then who does? The answer is that parents and society do. How, you ask? Children grow up watching the way their parents behave. They also observe the habits of people in the media, teachers, neighbors, and extended family members and eventually imitate the things they see. Someone once said that children are like video cameras with legs. They walk around recording everything we say and do.

Parents teach us how to walk, talk, eat, and negotiate our way through life. They teach us how to interact with our world. They teach us the difference between right and wrong and good and bad. While many parents serve as wonderful role models, some parents are capable of teaching their offspring how to cheat, lie, fornicate, abuse, steal, disrespect marriage, mistreat others, be hypocritical, hate themselves, or disregard the law.

Parents don't have to verbalize to their children what they think. Their silent testimony, the manner in which they conduct their lives, illustrates what is acceptable to them. They might not say, "Hey, why don't you become a drug addict when you grow up?" or "Why not become a fornicator or an alcoholic?" But if their lifestyles are dysfunctional, they convey to their children by example what is acceptable.

By now I'm sure you're asking, *What does family dysfunction have to do with idol worship?* The answer is: more than we think. Idol worship isn't simply muttering some ritual on bended knee. It entails much more than the adoration of a wood carving that we place on a shelf or in the center of a shrine. An idol can be anything we fervently pursue instead of God.

An idol is something we *regularly, consistently,* and *habitually* seek that brings gratification or a high in a time of need, hurt, or anxiety. Simply put, it is anything that replaces the Lord God Almighty in our lives. At the core of the human heart is the need to worship something. When God isn't the center of our lives, we focus our adoration on something or someone who makes us feel better. That could mean bowing down and worshiping statues. Or it could be the unquenchable hunger for material wealth. Perhaps it's an addiction. All idols have one thing in common: they are things or people we bond to and become dependent upon. They are almost impossible to live without.

For alcoholics, liquor becomes an idol because they find strength through liquid courage. They seek to calm the voices of anxiety in their heads from the daily pressures they face. And when they find simulated tranquility in the face of the screaming demons that haunt them, that's when alcohol becomes their god.

In our culture, compulsive buying is perhaps the biggest vice. Now more than ever, people overspend as a way to fill the void in their hearts. Shopping in the twenty-first century has turned into a relentless pursuit of acquiring that specific article of clothing, electronic device, household appliance, new car, video game, or the latest model of whatever we think will fill that empty spot in our lives. When we habitually seek a material object instead of God to fill the void in our hearts, we are participating in idolatry.

The same can be said about drugs. More and more people turn to mood-altering substances to combat feelings of loneliness and anxiety. This habit can easily lead to a dangerous dependency, and their bodies become physically addicted to the substance. Perhaps the drug addict doesn't bow down and worship a god called cocaine. But many addicts are willing to kill for the substance that gives them temporary relief. Over time, it becomes their god.

Whether it is looking at pornography, abusing others, habitually lying, consistently engaging in gossip, committing frequent acts of adultery, eating for the wrong reasons, or watching too much television, anything can become an idol. We are capable of worshiping anything in our time of need. And if we allow ourselves to worship these things as idols, we enslave ourselves and teach the sinful behavior to the generations that follow us.

Recent studies indicate that children with at least one parent who drinks is four times more likely to become alcoholics themselves. They are more likely to use other drugs, develop eating disorders, and become suicidal. They are twice as likely to marry alcoholics.[1] This pattern of destruction is not limited to drinking. Other habits can have devastating consequences as well. But the one thing wrong behaviors all have in common is the ease by which they can be learned and passed on to the next generation, the children.

Someone might say, *Just because I drink, my kids won't necessarily become alcoholics.* Or, *Just because I'm a compulsive shopper* [or food addict] *doesn't guarantee my kids will develop the same habits*. True!

But if you knew that building your house on the shoulder of an interstate highway would quadruple the likelihood that your child would be killed by a car, would you build your home there? Why play the percentages? Why take the chance of negatively affecting the three or four generations that follow?

THERE'S A BETTER PLAN

Instead of continuing in the same vicious pattern of behavior you've seen in previous generations, why not stop it? You can experience true freedom from the things that hold you back. Whether you struggle with a vice or compulsive behavior or simply feel stuck, God offers you the power to break the chains. He offers you power through Christ.

We will now focus our attention on what Christ came to do, His mission. Then, once we have a clear idea of what He can do in our lives, we will discover several keys to freedom from destructive cycles in our lives.

It was a sunny day, not a cloud in the sky. Jesus, God's Son, traveled to the town where He was raised. That Sabbath morning, the synagogue was packed. He stood in front of the chair where the rabbis gave their discourses. Suddenly, the attendant walked toward the front and handed Him the scroll written by the prophet Isaiah. Jesus quickly moved His finger down the text and found the exact portion that spelled out His mission. The crowd began to hush. After quick examination, Jesus raised His head, looked at His audience, and said:

> The Spirit of the Lord is on me,
>   because he has anointed me
> to preach good news to the poor.
>   He has sent me to proclaim freedom for
>   the prisoners
> and recovery of sight for the blind,
>   to release the oppressed,
> to proclaim the year of the Lord's favor.
>
> (Luke 4:18)

With a subtle nod, He signaled the attendant to take the scroll back. He sat down and looked over the audience. Every eye focused on him. Then He made the declaration that changed history: "Today this scripture is fulfilled in your hearing" (Luke 4:21).

At that moment Jesus announced that God had sent Him to deliver those who were spiritually oppressed. Every person caught in the clutches of sinful and destructive patterns could experience a new life. That word applied not only to Jesus' audience two thousand years ago but to us today. More important, that word applies to you. If you are poor (in any way, not just financially) and need good news, in prison (stuck in any bad habit) and desire freedom, blind and want to see, or oppressed and looking for deliverance, Christ offers you His powerful helping hand to set you free.

Whether your parents were abusive, divorced, or addicted to a substance, that cycle does not have to continue in your life. Maybe past generations have nothing to do with it. You might be the one who is starting a cycle of craziness. Either way, it doesn't have to continue. It doesn't have to be passed on to the next generation. You don't have to become like the person who raised you.

This is what happens when we choose God's plan: our lives change, and our families' lives change. His plan not only enables us to break the chains upon our lives, but as we obey the laws He laid out in Exodus and continue to partner with Him through prayer, we set in motion the blessing that touches a thousand generations that follow us.

Just as the Lord dedicated a verse to describe the consequences of having idols, He also gave us a verse that describes the ramifications of being obedient to His law. The last verse of the passage we examined earlier talks about what God does for those who obey Him. Exodus 20:6 says He shows "love to a thousand generations of those who love me and keep my commandments." Christ was sent to help us develop a relationship with God, to love Him, and keep His commandments. And when we keep His commandments, we and our families begin to experience the blessings of God for many generations.

Now, we'll look at some ways to break destructive cycles.

KEYS TO BREAKING DESTRUCTIVE CYCLES

1. Breaking the Cycle Begins with a Constant Transfer of Leadership

Once we discover the origins of the things that hold us back, we engage in a constant transfer of leadership from us to God. I use the phrase *constant transfer* because our human nature pushes us to be the leaders of our own lives. There will always be a tendency to do the things *we* want to do. That struggle is something everyone faces, especially when it comes to the battle of doing what is godly or sinful. It's a tug of war between what we want and what God says is right. Paul understood this well. He admitted, "I decide to do good, but I don't really do it; I decide not to do bad, but then I do it anyway. My decisions, such as they are, don't result in actions. Something has gone wrong deep within me and gets the better of me every time" (Rom. 7:19–20 *The Message*).

You might be thinking, *I have a relationship with God. I go to church once in a while. I even read my Bible and pray from time to time. Why should I transfer leadership of my life to God every day?* Believe me, friend, all of these things are wonderful and will benefit you in more ways than you can imagine. But just because we attend church, read our Bibles, and pray does not mean that we are automatically freed from destructive behavior. Initiating a relationship with God is a great place to start, but that's only where the process of gaining freedom begins. The constant transfer of leadership must continue each day until we die.

I've counseled thousands of people who attend church and say they have a relationship with God. In the next breath, they tell me about their struggle with pornography, drinking, drugs, or something else. These habits steal their joy. Do they know God? Sure. Are they free? Obviously not. It's one thing to know God as Savior and Lord. It's another thing to align your priorities according to His will.

That is precisely why Jesus said, "Anyone who intends to come with me has to let me lead. You're not in the driver's seat—I am. Don't run from suffering; embrace it. Follow me and I'll show you how" (Luke 9:23 *The Message*). Making Christ Lord of our lives is a daily process, one that requires that we take our selfish agenda and put it to one side. Then we can say, "Be Lord in my life, and give me Your power to reinvent myself."

Recently, I met with someone who read my first book, *Breaking the Barriers*. I'll call him John. The thirty-five-year-old ex-stockbroker had a stellar record throughout his career. During the span of two decades, he moved up the ranks. And John had a happy personal life. He was married and attended church regularly.

One day, the company called for an investigation, and the stress became overwhelming for John. Although John was deemed innocent of any wrongdoing during the investigation, he took a leave of absence. Within weeks, his conditioned worsened, and he became depressed.

Between the stress and depression, his sense of right and wrong began to deteriorate. Instead of turning to alcohol or drugs, John headed toward the dangerous waters of Internet pornography. He began crossing a moral line. Of course, his wife didn't know about his secret. No one in the church suspected anything. His friends never thought to ask.

At first, his habit took him to mainstream porno-graphic websites, but when they no longer satisfied his desire for erotic pleasure, he navigated to sites with underage girls. Soon, he was chatting online with young teenagers. Christ was no longer at the helm of his heart. John had chosen an idol and transferred leadership back to his own command. His moral compass wasn't just malfunctioning, it was completely destroyed.

One day he met a junior high cheerleader in an online chat room. Her name was Brianna. He told her that he was a sophomore in high school, playing junior varsity football. At first, their conversation was super-ficial, but after ten days, she began to open up to him. She was distraught over the fact that her parents had gotten a divorce and that her mother allowed some guy she barely knew to move in with them. Over the course of several weeks, they chatted every night into the early hours of the morning. Finally, he revealed his desire to meet her face-to-face. She agreed.

They arranged a time and agreed upon a specific place. He didn't want to be too conspicuous, so he waited fifteen minutes before arriving at the rendez-vous location, a secluded area with tables behind a building adjacent to a park. He walked down the corridor between the two buildings and rounded the corner. There she was, a young lady sitting alone at one of the tables. His heart was racing. She was more beautiful than the picture she had e-mailed him. As he approached, he said, "Are you Brianna?" She said, "Why? Who wants to know?" He said, "It's me, John." Just as he said his name, someone grabbed him from behind and said, "You're under arrest!"

Before he knew it, he was pinned to the ground by two undercover cops who then read him his rights. The girl sitting at the table was a police officer, a decoy. Unbeknownst to John, he actually had been conversing in a chat room with a thirty-five-year-old man who was part of a special task force to catch sexual predators.

A man who had a distinguished Wall Street career, a beautiful marriage, and a promising future suddenly found himself behind bars for something unimaginable. He spent his time in jail thinking about the mistakes he had made. The most tragic mistake was pushing his relationship with God to one side and embracing his own agenda. That mistake brought about his demise. Up until his arrest, he gradually took back the throne of his own heart, and rejected the leadership of Christ. As a result, sinful patterns destroyed everything he loved and cherished.

He heard good Bible teaching, read his Bible, and

prayed. But when it came time to align his priorities with the will of God, he fell miserably short. Sitting in jail, he decided to reconnect with God. Unfortunately, he had to do so alone, without a wife or family. He painfully discovered the devastating consequences of idol worship and trying to run his own life.

If we want to experience freedom from the patterns that bring destruction upon us, the first key is to transfer leadership to God. Embracing His lordship enables us to move through the confusing maze of things that hold us back. Allowing Christ to help us define what is right and wrong will always point our lives in the right direction. If we don't have Christ as our leader, we won't know which direction to take and we'll flounder in indecision. Our destructive habits will become the next generation's destructive habits.

Is being leader of your own life leading to a healthy, happy life? If not, perhaps you need to give leadership of your life to God. If you are experiencing difficulty in choosing between what is right or wrong, there is good news. God wants to help. When you give Christ leadership over your heart, the destructive cycle breaks and the power of the kingdom of God is released in your life. No vice can hold you. No chain is too strong. No adversary can overtake you. When your heart is in God's hands, He is on your side. "So, what do you think? With God on our side like this, how can we lose?" (Rom. 8:31 *The Message*). The answer is, we can't.

When you yield your will to His, God will finish the work of blessing that He begins in you. "There has never been the slightest doubt in my mind that the God who started this great work in you would keep at it and bring it to a flourishing finish on the very day Christ Jesus appears" (Phil. 1:6 *The Message*). As long as you desire, God will work to keep you going in the right direction. As long as you seek His will and His leadership each day, you will be moving toward God's best for you.

Maybe you know Christ as Savior and Lord, but when you face a particular temptation, you find yourself struggling. If that's the case the next key in breaking the cycle promises to be helpful as you tap into God's power to reinvent yourself.

2. Breaking the Cycle Begins by Dealing with Temptation

It was one of the darkest nights of my life. Four years after I decided to follow Christ in that old Christian Missionary Alliance Church in Big Bear Lake, I slowly walked away from my relationship with Him. I was a junior in college. Unfortunately, I hadn't dealt with the baggage from my childhood. I began to live a life that was incongruent with my Christian values, and as a result, I couldn't get the upper hand with the temptations I faced.

One night, I drank too much champagne mixed with another substance, all on an empty stomach. Within minutes, I had a horrific sensation that I had lost my mind and all sense of time. It was as though I was living in a parallel universe.

Panic gripped my heart and wouldn't let go. My tongue dropped to the back of my throat, and my heart began to race. I tried to take slow, deep breaths, but nothing worked. No matter what I told myself, I couldn't calm down. Finally I asked a friend to drive me to the emergency room.

The doctor read my chart, took one look at me and said, "Why would a bright young man like you do such a foolish thing? You're better than that. You won't try that again, will you?"

"No, sir," I said. And I meant it.

He turned and headed to the door, saying, "You'll be fine in an hour or so."

I was speechless. His rebuke was convicting and to the point. What a foolish thing I had done. The sad thing was, I knew better, but I let temptation get the best of me. Within an hour or so, things started to settle down in my head.

I made a sobering discovery through that painful episode. Without Christ, we are helpless to break free from the patterns that keep us in captivity. Without a relationship with God, we lack the power necessary to overcome the things that hold us back. Without God's help, it's extremely difficult to overcome the temptations we face. I needed His power to resist, but my relationship with God had deteriorated, and with it my ability to say no.

The Bible says in 1 Peter 5:8, "Be self-controlled and alert. Your enemy the devil prowls around like a roaring lion looking for someone to devour." Satan labors endlessly to lure us to compromise the laws that God handed to humanity. And he knows our weaknesses. Satan puts temptations in our paths to bring about our demise. Once we are ruined, we show other generations how to follow suit.

Have you ever been on a diet? It can be a painful experience, especially for the first week or two. Allow me to create a scenario. Let's say you start off great. You muster the willpower to increase your daily activities and lower your caloric intake. You have been going to the gym four times a week and successfully avoiding chocolate bars, fried foods, and twenty-ounce frappuccinos. One day, you get a call from a friend inviting you to a dinner at her home. You accept the invitation but cautiously mention that you are trying to diet.

When you arrive, in addition to your host's smile, you notice the enticing aroma of pesto chicken and garlic bread. You walk through the living room and admire the candlelit atmosphere. It's ideal for a nice, friendly dinner. Her attention to detail is impeccable. You sit down at the table with the other guests. The first bite of chicken is incredible, and now you sense that you're in trouble. The portions are small, but you decide to have an extra helping. After all, it is only chicken. The fruit drink is unbelievable. But hey, drinks don't count. Right? You wave your host on as if to say, *Just keep pouring*! While you are at it, you scoop up an extra helping of the cheese broccoli. After all, it is a vegetable.

Then your host brings out the dessert. It happens to be your favorite dessert, a chocolate-coffee mud pie made with ice cream baptized in hot fudge sauce. Suddenly, the world stops. Is that your imagination? Or is that a saxophone playing smooth jazz in the background? As your friend places this monstrosity of a temptation on the table, you notice the toasted slivered almonds that blanket the outer edges. The voice reminding you how fat you felt when you started the diet has been silenced.

Your clothes do not seem to fit as tight now. You think, *Maybe I'll just have half a piece.* So you go to work slowly on the half portion. The table talk goes on and on. People are joyful. The conversation is light. Unfortunately, no one clears the table, and you try not to stare at the remaining portions of the pie. But you cannot help it. It's as though the other half of your piece begins to speak to you: *Here I sit, all alone, waiting to bring someone immeasurable pleasure. Come on. Don't let me go to waste.*

You can't stop yourself. You grab your fork and stab the other half of the piece that you left on the serving tray. Besides, it was *your* piece. After several minutes, you shave off yet another piece. Before you get up from the table, you've consumed more calories than you have in the past two days. The damage is done.

In this scenario, you fell into temptation not because of steamed vegetables or broiled fish. You fell, first of all, because something tempted you. It played to your weakness, and it enticed you. Second, you were unable to see the consequences of your actions until it was too late, that is, until you stepped on the scale the next morning. Had you known in advance that your total intake that night would be close to two thousand calories, you might have preferred to meet your friend for coffee.

Satan tempts people in similar ways. While mud pie may not destroy our life or family, things like an extramarital affair, drug addiction, or overspending certainly can. The enemy promises pleasure, power, fun, and excitement. Unfortunately, we cannot see what it costs us until it's too late. In the midst of temptation, we have difficulty hearing the voice of reason, the voice of goodness, the voice of righteousness, the voice that helps us make healthy choices for our loved ones and ourselves. Every time temptation leads us to break one of God's laws, we stand on the scale of life and sadly come to grips with the damage that was done.

Do you need to experience victory over the things that pull you down? Do you need to discover a powerful way to overcome temptation? Do you need to develop self-control? If so, the following story promises to reveal some powerful tools you can use to overcome the temptations that pull you down.

In Matthew 3:13–17, we find this story: The air was crisp. The skies were blue and not a cloud was in sight. Jesus made His way down to the river. Just as He approached the shore, He saw a man named John baptizing people in the Jordan. When Jesus asked him to be baptized, John said, "I need to be baptized by you." Jesus insisted, "Let it be so now; it is proper for us to do this to fulfill all righteousness" (v. 15). In his heart, John knew that Jesus was right.

Just as soon as Jesus came out of the water, He saw the Spirit of God descending like a dove, and a celestial glow rested on Him. Suddenly, everyone heard a voice from heaven saying, "This is my Son, whom I love; with him I am well pleased" (v. 17).

No sooner had He heard those words than the Spirit led Him into the desert for a time of ministerial preparation. For forty days, Jesus ate nothing, and by the time the sixth week of fasting had ended, He was hungry. That's when the devil came to tempt Him. His timing was not coincidental.

Knowing what was at stake, the enemy decided to tempt Jesus in an area that He would eventually have to surrender. He couldn't go on forever without food and water. Sooner or later the fast had to come to an end and Satan knew it. Perhaps all Jesus needed was a simple nudge to fall off the wagon. There was a subtle challenge beneath the culinary temptation. Satan would challenge His ego as well. His words were strategic and calculated.

"If you are the Son of God, tell these stones to become bread" (Matt. 4:3). The challenge implied that the enemy doubted Christ's deity. If Jesus was the Son of God, He wouldn't need to turn stones into bread.

If He wasn't the Son of God, perhaps Satan could give Him something to eat. The enemy was probably expecting an answer like, "What do you mean, '*If* I am'?" Or "Boy, I sure am hungry, I could go for a nice baguette right now."

Rather than engage in a debate, though, Jesus quoted Scripture. "It is written: 'Man does not live on bread alone, but on every word that comes from the mouth of God'" (Matt. 4:4). God was His strength, and He got plenty of nourishment through the time He spent with His heavenly Father.

The enemy showed no discouragement. Instead, he led Jesus to the heart of the holy city, and with one powerful move, lifted him to the pinnacle of the temple. In their first encounter, Jesus used Scripture as a strong defense. This time, Satan would not be outdone. Opening with the same line as before, Satan said, "If you are the Son of God,...throw yourself down. For it is written: 'He will command his angels concerning you, and they will lift you up in their hands, so that you will not strike your foot against a stone'" (v. 6). This time, Satan tested Jesus' vanity. Once again, Jesus answered by quoting Scripture. "It is also written: 'Do not put the Lord your God to the test'" (v. 7). There was no need for further debate or elaboration.

Satan was determined to find a crack in Jesus'

armor. After testing His ego, vanity, and physical needs, what was left? Could a man resist all the splendor, glory, and power in the world? Surely these things would be enough to tempt Christ. This time, Satan chose not to taunt His deity. Instead, he took Jesus to a high mountain where they could see all the kingdoms of the world in their splendor. "All this I will give you," Satan said, "if you will bow down and worship me" (Matt. 4:9).

Once again, Christ's soul was not for sale, at any price. Satan's offer was instantly rejected. The deal was entirely offensive, and with a voice of authority Christ said to the devil, "Away from me, Satan! For it is written: 'Worship the Lord your God, and serve him only'" (Matt. 4:10). The challenge was over. Jesus resisted, and the enemy could do only one thing—flee. Then God sent angels to attend to His Son's needs.

Jesus overcame because there was a line He would not cross. In His mind, it was never an option. He didn't let His ego get in the way. He didn't allow vanity to lure Him to do something He would later regret. He didn't let His thirst for power seduce Him into selling His soul. He rejected the notion that His physical needs superseded His spiritual ones.

Unfortunately, some people are willing to sacrifice their dignity in order to obtain power. Others are willing to do anything for money. Still other individuals compromise their values because they insist on looking out for number one.

So what can we learn from Christ's example about handling temptation? First, we need to define in our minds which line we will never cross. Whether it's cheating on our spouses, deliberately trying to deceive someone, or using words to harm others, we must clearly outline the areas that we consider unacceptable. Once they become clear, then we can begin to build up resistance to the things that demonstrate power over us.

Next, we can learn to use Scripture to address our weaknesses. When temptation rises, we can let the Lord fight the battle as we use His Word to speak to the matter. Jesus had one-sentence answers to Satan's temptations that were biblical and to the point. He didn't engage in a debate or get distracted.

Finally, in the last encounter, Christ issued a sharp rebuke to Satan to leave him. Sometimes temptation won't let up, and it constantly chips away at our defenses. That's when we simply need to raise our voice and say, "Enough is enough, away from me, Satan!" Sometimes we need to take the authority that Christ offers us and use it. The Bible says, "The seventy-two returned with joy and said, 'Lord, even the demons submit to us in your name.' He replied, 'I saw Satan fall like lightning from heaven. I have given you authority to trample on snakes and scorpions and to overcome all the power of the enemy; nothing will harm you'" (Luke 10:17–19).

Finally, the best way to deal with temptation is to ask God for the strength to resist it. "Submit yourselves, then, to God. Resist the devil, and he will flee from you" (James 4:7). Remember, you are not alone. God is with you, and He understands the things you are facing. "For we do not have a high priest who is unable to sympathize with our weaknesses," the Bible says, "but we have one who has been tempted in every way, just as we are—yet was without sin. Let us then approach the throne of grace with confidence, so that we may receive mercy and find grace to help us in our time of need" (Heb. 4:15–16). The next time you face a difficult temptation, know that God will guide you through the storm and give you the power to overcome the things that tempt you.

So far in this section we covered two important keys in breaking the cycle. We have studied the importance of constantly transferring the leadership of our lives to the Lord and learning how to handle temptation. Now we are going to focus on the third key.

3. Breaking the Cycle Begins with Being Aware of What You Say, Feel, and Do

To escape the cycle of destructive behavior in our lives, we must pay attention to our words, our feelings, and our behavior. Let's look first at the importance of the words we speak.

What you say. I admire and respect Zig Ziglar, one of the better communicators of our day. In one of his audio series, he makes a profound statement: "Remember, the microphone is always on." He is right. Someone is always listening to what we say. Our words never go unheard. Even when we think we are completely alone, the Lord is always with us and hears our thoughts before they are spoken (Ps. 139:2, 7).

The way we speak has a great impact on our loved ones, especially our children. If we want to break the cycle of destruction in our marriage and family, we need to be aware of the things we say and the way we say them. Every word carries a meaning and an impression. Once it escapes our mouth, we can't take it back.

☙

It had been a long speaking tour, and I was glad to be heading home. I left Miami first thing in the morning with one stop. Knowing that I would soon see my family, I could handle one final leg to Los Angeles. After landing, I discovered that my final flight was delayed four hours. *That can't be*, I thought. I wanted to see my wife and girls. And I was looking forward to sleeping in my own bed. I didn't want to spend one more second than I had to away from home.

After standing in line for thirty minutes, I was transferred to another flight. Finally, I was heading home. What a great feeling! I sat down in the seat overlooking the right engine. The plane backed away from the gate and started to taxi down the runway. I tuned in to a channel on the audio system of the aircraft dedicated to air traffic control. On it, passengers could listen to the conversations between the pilot and the control tower. During takeoff I heard the pilot make a startling statement. He called the tower and said, "Uh, we have a problem. During takeoff, our right front windshield cracked. I think we need to return to the airport immediately."

Fear gripped me. We were approaching ten thousand feet and could not go any higher until it was decided if we were continuing or returning to the airport. The control tower asked the pilot what he wanted to do. He responded, "Well, we are not sure if there are any operation restrictions while flying with a cracked windshield. We're calling our headquarters. Please stand by."

I do not consider myself a paranoid flyer. I enjoy flying. However, I was visualizing the air pressure within the plane causing the windshield to explode. If that happened, the pilot would be sucked out of the aircraft along with the rest of the crew and 140 passengers. That seemed a reasonable concern, especially since the pilot wouldn't ascend higher than ten thousand feet.

Somehow, the audio channel was patched into all the communications of the cockpit. I heard two telephone rings followed by three ascending tones. Then I heard the phrase that we all loathe, "We're sorry, all circuits are busy. Please try your call again later." *I can't believe what I am hearing!* I thought.

Meanwhile, we continued in a holding pattern at ten thousand feet.

Again, the phone rang twice—followed by the same recording. Finally, on the third attempt, I heard the dispatcher answer. He managed to reach the maintenance supervisor, and after several long minutes, all three were having a conference call. The maintenance supervisor searched his manual for the section on cracked windshields.

He asked, "Which windshield has the crack, the inside or outside pane?" I was thinking, *Who cares? Just land the plane!* "We believe it's the outside window that's cracked," the pilot answered. "Well, if that is the case, there are no operational restrictions. However, as soon as you land, the aircraft will be grounded until maintenance can replace the entire windshield. That will take about eight hours." The pilot thanked the supervisor and hung up.

Then he called the control tower, which had been guiding us through the dozens of planes arriving into and leaving the area. The pilot said, "Well, it looks like we have no operational restrictions. However, we have burned up more fuel than we anticipated by circling for the past fifteen minutes. I am not sure we have enough fuel to make it to Los Angeles."

"What do you want to do?" asked the controller. After several long seconds, the pilot answered, "We'll go until we run out of gas, I mean as far as we can. I think we'll head for Los Angeles."

Excuse me, I thought. *Am I the only one who thinks this is a bad idea?* Flying with a cracked windshield sounded like a disaster in the making. Then we discovered that the crew didn't know if we had enough gas to get there. Flying is not like driving a car. We can't simply pull off the freeway and fill-er-up if we get a little low. There are hardly any places to land a Boeing 737 until you reach Las Vegas. When I heard the words, "We'll go as far as we can," I was less anxious to sleep in my own bed and more eager to feel the ground—any ground—under my feet.

The rest of the flight was smooth and uneventful. The pilot made wise choices along the way, and our lives were never in danger. Obviously, we made it to Los Angeles in one piece. Favorable winds and air-traffic conditions allowed us to arrive only twenty minutes late. Once we landed, I thanked God. Then I met my family for dinner and treasured the moment all the more.

Although the captain and first officer were highly skilled individuals, they didn't take into account the impact their words would have on those of us in the main cabin. The microphone was on the whole time, but the two guys flying the plane were clueless. Every passenger listening to the audio channel heard what was said and the tone in which it was said. As we approached Los Angeles, the flight attendant called the flight deck and told the captain that the passengers heard the transmissions between the plane, the control tower, and the maintenance hangar. To that, he replied something I cannot repeat here!

Wisdom tells us that there will always be an audience listening to what we say and that our words have a powerful impact on the lives of others. Our children are constantly tuning in. Our families pick up every subtle tone and nuance that slips out of our mouths. Our friends sit in the main cabin of life listening to everything going on in the cockpit. David knew the importance of watching his words. He said, "I will watch my ways and keep my tongue from sin" (Ps. 39:1).

Why is this point so vital in breaking the cycle of destructive behaviors? Because a father can drastically affect his daughter's self-esteem with one comment about her weight. A mother can damage her son's fragile ego with one sly comment about his lack of intelligence. A husband can create an atmosphere of loneliness in his marriage by using hardly any words. A wife can push her husband away by using too many. "Likewise the tongue is a small part of the body, but it makes great boasts. Consider what a great forest is set on fire by a small spark. The tongue also is a fire, a world of evil among the parts of the body. It corrupts the whole person, sets the whole course of his life on fire, and is itself set on fire by hell" (James 3:5–6).

Perhaps the most important reason we need to be aware of our words is that what we speak is a strong indication of the things we keep in our hearts. How we view people, especially our family members, will eventually come out in our words. That's why Jesus warned his disciples about the way they spoke to one another. He said, "The things that come out of the mouth come from the heart, and these make a man 'unclean'" (Matt. 15:18). Sooner or later, we verbalize the way we perceive our children, spouse, brothers, sisters, and others close to us. What we say can be hurtful or it can be uplifting. The choice is ours. One of the ways we can work diligently to break the cycle of destructive behavior is to be conscious of what we say.

With our words, we can build up people and inspire them to break the barriers that hold them back. In doing so, we will move one step closer to breaking the cycle that keeps us from moving forward. Monitoring our words is only a portion of the process. In many ways, what we say is directly connected to the way we feel. This brings us to the next area of awareness, understanding what we feel.

What you feel. The greatest adversary we face in breaking the cycle of destruction may not be what we've experienced. It might not be our past or some trauma we witnessed. It could be, in fact, our emotions, the way we feel. You see, many people are unaware of their emotions and the power they have over us. Do you know a woman who is involved in an unhealthy relationship with a man she knows isn't good for her? Yet because she feels lonely, she settles for less. After a year or two, she finally wonders why she wasted so much time on someone who only cares about himself. In this case, her feelings pushed her toward something unhealthy.

Be aware of what you feel. Take note of what your feelings are trying to say to you. If you ignore them, you might wind up like the woman in a bad relationship. Or perhaps you might become like the teenage girl who struggles with frequent thoughts of suicide. Or you might imitate the young athlete who has a promiscuous lifestyle. Feelings have an ironic way of manipulating us when we fail to recognize their presence.

People often seem to enjoy the destructive behaviors they are trying to change. But that is only partially true. Alcoholics don't drink because they enjoy the action of ingesting. Nor do shopaholics purchase because they enjoy swiping their credit cards and getting further in debt. Instead, people drink or shop because they are addicted to the feelings that those vices produce when they engage in their destructive behavior. Regardless of the dysfunction, people are addicted to the way they *feel* as a result of their interaction with the habit. They are attached to the things that bring them pleasure.[2]

There was a time when I tried to ignore some intense

emotions I felt that stemmed from the trauma of my childhood. I didn't feel comfortable with loneliness or sadness. Because I refused to deal with those emotions, I found myself in and out of relationships, looking for solace in a bottle of beer, or working overtime to earn my happiness. I began to live a life that was contrary to what I knew God wanted me to live. Doing those things helped me to silence the voices of loneliness in my head. They helped to distract me from the pain I felt. That's why the Lord warns us to vigilantly guard our emotions. "The heart is deceitful above all things and beyond cure. Who can understand it?" (Jer. 17:9). Our emotions have a powerful influence over us and can mislead us.

The next time you find yourself moving toward something you know is destructive, ask yourself: "What am I feeling right now? Do I feel hopeless, angry, hurt, resentful, or anxious?" If that is the case, look for a way to express it to the Lord. Ask God for help. You can always count on Him. In the midst of an emotionally turbulent world, He always is with us.

⤞❦⤝

It was a long night. My daughter Celina, just ten days old, could not sleep. I held her in my arms and rocked slowly in the chair trying to get her to fall asleep. At

3:00 in the morning, I decided to turn on the television. In the midst of a sea of infomercials I found a program about children who were recovering from physical abuse. As I watched it, suddenly Celina raised her head for a few seconds and gazed into my eyes.

As a father, I found it difficult to imagine why people would put their children in harm's way, let alone abuse them. As I alternately focused on the faces on the screen and my daughter's, a tear began to roll down my cheek. I remember silently saying to her, *As long as you live under my roof, you won't have to worry about that.* Although my daughter was safe, I realized many children would suffer from abuse, neglect, or abandonment. But children are not the only victims. Many teenagers and adults suffer abuse, and as a result endure feelings of depression and suicide.

When we are weighed down by feelings that overwhelm us and drive us to do things that are destructive, where can we turn? The Lord gives us a significant truth in the Bible. It's a verse that speaks to our hearts when we look for peace. It is perhaps the most important verse we can hold on to during our time of stress or emotional difficulty: "Cast all your anxiety on him because he cares for you" (1 Pet. 5:7).

We can take our feelings to the Lord, no matter what they are. That door is always open. God loves us. He wants to help us. He understands the tangle of emotion that we feel. When you feel out of control, remember this significant truth: regardless of whether you feel suicidal, depressed, or full of euphoria, God understands and accepts you just the way you are. As Scripture tells us, "Cast your cares on the LORD and he will sustain you; he will never let the righteous fall" (Ps. 55:22).

What you do. The final thing we must be aware of if we are to escape a cycle of destructive behavior is our behavior. Awareness leads to ownership, and ownership leads to personal responsibility. Instead of blaming our parents or family members, we need to take responsibility for our behavior and the results of our decisions. When we can admit that the things we do are destructive and are a result of our own choices, then half the battle is won. Recovery appears on the horizon.

⚬✵⚬

The doctor shook his head, removed the stethoscope from his ears, and took off the blood pressure cuff. He said, "Well, Mr. Frenn, we need to do something about that blood pressure." There I sat, all 235 pounds of me, wondering how a twenty-nine-year-old man could have high blood pressure. To make matters worse, my cholesterol was approaching three hundred. Granted, I was a chocoholic. I loved food, any kind of food, and I hardly exercised. Still, it didn't make sense, I thought.

In the doctor's office, I was faced with reality. I had to admit there was a problem, and I couldn't run from it. I couldn't ignore the elephant in the room—*I* was the elephant. That's when I decided to do something about the cycle of destruction in my life. After all, my dad had a heart attack when he was fifty-seven. Both of my grandfathers died from cardiac arrest, one at age fifty-five, the other at forty-nine. If I was going to break this ominous cycle, I had to start working on it now. Like the phrase I mentioned earlier, I discovered my *why*: I didn't want to die before my time. In that sense, I definitely didn't want to become like my father or grandfathers.

I understood that most of the responsibility for changing rested with me. I had to take ownership for my own actions. No one else was to blame. My own conduct and actions had brought this upon me. As the Bible warns, "Do not be deceived: God cannot be mocked. A man reaps what he sows. The one who sows to please his sinful nature, from that nature will reap destruction; the one who sows to please the Spirit, from the Spirit will reap eternal life" (Gal. 6:7–8).

How many thousands of pounds of food did I consume for pure pleasure? How many years did I live in a fantasy?

So I asked the Lord to help me. I knew if I partnered with God, He would be faithful. I also knew that if I could manage to be faithful, the benefits would be great. "Let us not become weary in doing good," Scripture encourages us, "for at the proper time we will reap a harvest if we do not give up" (Gal. 6:9).

That summer of 1996, the Olympics were held in Atlanta. For two weeks, the U.S. Olympic team collected medals. Sprinter Michael Johnson won several gold medals in his "gold Nikes." Johnson was about my age, so I watched the replays of his victories with interest. That's when the thought hit me: *If he can become one of the fastest men in the world, I can get in shape*!

My priority was not to lose weight. Losing weight is only one indicator that the body is in shape. Rather, my goal was to have a healthy lifestyle and a healthy body. In order to reach that goal, I first had to find the source of the destructive pattern I had developed.

What was the root of my problem? I was unaware of how much I was consuming each day. I thought, *I don't eat junk food. I don't eat that much.* In the same way, we can be unaware of how much money we spend until the end of the month. So instead of guessing how much I consumed each day, I carried a small note pad with me and began to write down everything I ate. At the end of the day, I added up all the calories, fat grams, and sugar. I wasn't just surprised at the total, I was blown away!

Once I became aware of what I was doing, I decided to address what I wasn't doing.

I grabbed an old pair of tennis shoes. I put on my only workout shirt with "Just Do It" and the notorious *swoosh* on the front. About 7:00 each morning, I exercised for twenty minutes. I confess it was a painful beginning. I was convinced during the first two weeks I was going to die of a heart attack. Motivation was difficult. Each morning, I would get up and sit on the edge of the bed. At times, I sat there for ten minutes, staring at the floor, listening to my pillow invite me to return to Neverland. I learned an important lesson during that initial period of exercising. Motivation rarely comes before we act. Instead, it comes after we start acting. The more I exercised, the more I became motivated to do it.

After two months, a new habit began to emerge, one that changed my life for the better. I consumed fewer calories and ran three miles a day. I dropped sixty pounds and have kept it off since that time. That was over fourteen years ago. Now when I walk into my doctor's office, he simply says, "Whatever you're doing, Mr. Frenn, keep doing it."

I include this story because everywhere I go people want to know how I lost over 25 percent of my body weight. They want to know the secret formula for losing weight and getting in shape. My answer is always the same. I have no formula. I have something much more important. In my case, it wasn't just a desire for physical change. I had a need. It was a matter of life or death. I had a reason to change, a *why*, followed by an aha moment watching Michael Johnson in the Olympics.

Yes, I had to identify lines of temptation I wouldn't cross. I had to become aware of my thoughts and words. I had to become aware of feelings and how they played into eating patterns. There was an historical pattern that had to be broken, and God helped me to break it!

Friend, I believe that you are someone special. God loves you and cares deeply about you. He knows every person in your family who has struggled and He understands the desires of your heart to live a life full of freedom, peace, and harmony. I've prayed for you, even before you picked up this book. And of the many reasons I wrote this book, perhaps this one is the most important. I believe beyond the shadow of a doubt that God will help you break the patterns of destruction that keep you from moving forward! God will help you overcome and move past the things that hold you back.

In this chapter, we examined the patterns that are handed down from generation to generation and their impact on us. Christ has the power to help us break those destructive patterns that keep us from moving forward. He came to set the captives free. The three powerful keys—a constant transfer of leadership, learning to deal with temptation, and becoming aware of what we say, feel, and do—help us break the cycle and prepare us to walk in freedom.

⌘

As we bring this chapter to a close, I would like to suggest that you take a few moments to be alone with God. I trust that you will consider the following prayer as a guide as you ask God to help you break the destructive patterns in your life:

Dear Lord, thank You for sending Your Son, Jesus, to break the patterns of generational dysfunction in my life. I want to break the cycle that keeps me bound. Help me to experience

Your power when I feel weak. Help me to over-come the chains that have kept me from mov-ing forward.

Once again, I ask You for forgiveness. I know that I have not lived a perfect life. But right now I give my heart to You. Help me see the root of my problem. Help me understand where all this confusion stems from. Help me to once and for all derail those destructive pat-terns within me. I do not want to hand down this craziness to my children and coming gen-erations. Rather, I want to start a process of blessing for a thousand generations of those who love You and keep Your commandments.

I receive all that You have for me, and I receive Your power to reinvent myself. Pre-pare my heart for the great journey You have planned for me. Guide me, help me, and fill me with Your love. In Christ's name I pray. Amen.

CHAPTER 4

Form Godly Habits

—————— ⚭ ——————

I DON'T WANT TO BE with you anymore!" As Rick muttered those words from across the restaurant table, Evangeline felt her world collapsing. After nine years of marriage, the life she thought was so secure and beautiful was instantly shattered. The moment of awkward silence that followed the bombshell seemed to last forever.

Years before, Evangeline had been a brilliant student. She had attended Christian schools, gone to Christian universities, and had all Christian friends. She grew up as the daughter of a prominent pastor in a large church. In addition to having a warm personality and beautiful smile, her intelligence was matched by her deep compassion for others. She had the ability to make anyone feel special and interesting.

Two years after her college graduation, however, many of her friends moved away. Other friends began to focus on their marriages and on having children. They had little time for her. Her support system began to diminish. As a result, some of her convictions grew faint, and before she knew it, compromising her values became easy.

The same day she broke up with her fiancé, Evangeline traveled to a sales conference where she had a business meeting with Rick. Perhaps it was his wit, charming smile, tall muscular build, or his slight bad-boy disposition, but several minutes into their meeting, she knew she was in trouble. The attraction was intense. What was supposed to be a business trip turned out to be a romantic encounter in Palm Desert. Within weeks, she moved into his condo, and after five months, they eloped to Las Vegas.

Her parents were devastated. Her friends were shocked. Everyone except Evangeline thought she had lost her perspective. She drifted away from the moral convictions she developed as a child. Yet, in spite of it all, the seeds of godliness were there waiting for the right moment to sprout once again.

Rick's upbringing was completely different. He had

lived a promiscuous lifestyle from an early age. For a time, he struggled with drugs but eventually overcame his vice. He developed into a successful businessman, living life to the fullest and enjoying luxurious vacations each year. Outwardly, he had it all—a nice home and a wardrobe that would make any young entrepreneur envious. By the time he and Evangeline met, the thirty-two-year-old Jewish man was twice divorced and had two children from a previous marriage.

For six years, the couple faced waves of challenges but always managed to bob back to the surface. Together, they had a wonderful son, Jacob.

On September 11, 2001, families all over the world were drawn together to watch the horrific scenes of planes hitting the twin towers. Rick's family went over to be with Evangeline, but the one person missing in the group was Rick. He didn't come home, which Evangeline felt was odd. Rick had been distant and seemed consistently preoccupied and distracted. So she thought, *I probably haven't been paying enough attention to my husband, especially now that we've got a toddler. Perhaps it's time to start dating my husband again.* So she circled September 20 on the calendar and asked him out on a date.

The couple entered the low-lit restaurant and sat down at a table for two. After a few minutes of small talk, she began to experience an overwhelming impression. Trying to fight it for several minutes, she finally asked him if there was another woman in his life. "Are you having an affair?"

"No," he said, laughing off her inquisition.

Deep inside, she knew something wasn't right. The impression grew. *Ask him again!* She wondered if it was God's voice, curiosity, or simply paranoia. But she mustered up the courage. Raising her head ever so slightly, she asked, "Is there someone else?"

This time, Rick gave no response.

Evangeline's blue eyes widened.

After several moments of silence, one word slipped out of his mouth, "Yes."

After his disclosure came the most disheartening revelation. Rick hadn't been unfaithful only once. For nearly four years, he had various affairs with other women. And after the truth had been revealed, Rick said, "I don't want to be with you anymore. I don't want to be married. I'm done. I want out!" Similar to the catastrophic events Evangeline had watched on television nine days before on September 11, 2001, her own world came crashing down.

Until that point, Rick had justified his actions. As Evangeline focused her attention on their son, Rick felt neglected. *I have needs, too,* he thought. *She never leaves me notes in my coffee cup any more, hardly kisses me in public or goes out of her way to hold my hand.* He knew that she was a good mother, but he went off to work, earned the money, and looked for adventure. As long as he could keep that part of his life separate and hidden, there was no conflict in his mind.

When the couple arrived home that evening, Evangeline disappeared into her bedroom and desperately began to search her soul. For a decade she had lived the way she wanted, and it turned out to be disastrous. She wondered, *Am I going to lose everything—my son, my house, my marriage, my life?* Her world was a mess, but she knew that God was the only one who had the power to put her life back together again. She called her father, and together they prayed. Falling on her knees, she cried out to God and turned her life over to the Lord once again. Her commitment was not halfhearted, but immediate and genuine. And God heard her cry.

She also committed to find a church, because she knew she needed the support of others. Three days later, she walked into a local church. As a pastor's kid, she never sat in the front, but this time was different. She took a seat in the first row, and the pastor began to share a timely message: "Finding the Strength to

Go On." Every word the pastor spoke found its way to her heart. Tears streamed down her face during the entire message.

Indeed, God was speaking to her, and the message was loud and clear: God loved her. He cared about her. He forgave her and wanted to give her the strength to rebuild her devastated life. She no longer had to live exclusively under her own power. Instead, she could choose to embrace God's power to reinvent herself. Her first sigh of relief came during the message that day. She knew that God was going to take care of her. Although her life was seemingly out of control, God had it all under control.

Evangeline wasn't sure what to do about her broken marriage. One thing was clear, though. She had to work on her relationship with God. That was the starting point. Once her relationship with God was strong, the next steps for her marriage would become clear.

At first, Rick thought that her new commitment to God was a ploy to keep him from leaving. But when the weeks turned into months, he couldn't dismiss the dynamic change in her life. In November 2001, Rick came to Evangeline and said, "I've ended my relationship with the other person." He revealed to her that he wanted to reconcile with her.

She said, "I will stay with you on two conditions.

First, there will be no more inappropriate behavior. If there's a hint of anything whatsoever, I will take our son and leave."

Like most parents, Evangeline didn't want to pass on the mistakes she had made to her son. So she gave Rick the second condition: "I am going to raise our child as a believer in Christ. If you can accept those two conditions, I will stay in this marriage."

Rick agreed.

For three long years, Evangeline went the extra mile. She displayed a wonderful testimony of God's love to her husband and made a deliberate decision to forgive him. Many times, she would wait in bed until he fell asleep. Then she would go downstairs and cry for hours. She prayed many times, asking God to reach her husband and give her the strength to overcome the hurt. In the early hours of the morning, she would get up and crawl back into bed so that when he woke up, he would never know she had left. Every morning, Rick discovered a loving note in his coffee cup.

In January 2002, Evangeline and their son, Jacob, were getting ready for church on Saturday night. Rick came into the bedroom and asked, "Do you mind if I go to church with you tonight?" She immediately responded, "Of course, you are welcome to join us."

He was surprised to discover that the music was

nice and the people were friendly. The message was challenging yet practical. From that week forward, he began to attend church on a regular basis.

The couple also met with a small group each week. At first, Rick was skeptical, but the more questions he asked, the more he discovered that his assumptions had been faulty. He fervently searched for answers to questions like *Does God exist? Is there an eternity?* And he came to the conclusion in his own heart that indeed God does exist. This ultimately guided him to the most important decision of his life. On Good Friday 2005, at their church, Rick committed his heart to Christ and asked Him to be Lord of his life. That was the day Evangeline felt her wounded heart had been healed.

Rick's conversion was radical—he was baptized the following month and began attending a men's Bible study that met weekly. Today, he is a leader in their church, takes several missions trips a year, and together he and Evangeline host a couples' home group. His relationship with his wife and son has never been better. And most important, he has been *radically transformed by the power of God*. His transformation followed the change he saw in his wife. Seeing how God healed her pain and suffering opened the door of salvation for him.

Evangeline and Rick found the power to reinvent themselves. Evangeline took God's hand in the midst of a violent storm. When it seemed there was no hope, she fell on her knees and reached out to His power—the *only* power that can truly change hearts. She realized the mistakes she made and decided to turn her life over to God. She embraced God's perspective and extended His forgiveness to Rick. She then looked for a support system to help her stay the course. Similarly, Rick recognized that the life he was living was disastrous and made Christ Lord of his life. Rick has experienced a powerful transformation by the renewing of his mind. He spends time studying Scripture, fellowshiping with people of similar faith, and praying. He has formed a wonderful group of godly friends to help keep him from wandering off course. These are all things that God uses to transform us.

Up to this point, we have studied the initial steps in experiencing God's power to change. The process starts with a legitimate reason—our *why*—that motivates us to do something about changing our lives. Once we feel the need for change, we discover that a relationship with God changes our perceptions. Then we work with God to focus on what holds us back and to break those patterns of destruction.

In this chapter, we'll discuss forming godly habits

that inevitably produce incredible blessing, meaning, and significance in our lives. Once you put into practice the principles found in this chapter, you will experience a whole new level of freedom. I trust that you are ready to see powerful results in your life. If that's the case, let's lay the foundation for establishing godly patterns that lead us to victory.

CHANGE YOUR MIND-SET AND CHANGE YOUR DESTINY

Who we are and what we become is largely determined by the way we think. When we think godly thoughts, we can walk in the blessings of God. When we think ungodly thoughts, we walk in destruction. Many people have been told that they serve no good purpose, will never amount to anything, or will never lead a successful life—and they believe it. This is an ungodly way of thinking. Why? God doesn't want us to believe something about ourselves that isn't true. If we want to see God's power unleashed in our lives, we need to transform our thinking and take on the mind of Christ.

Having the mind of Christ simply means that we make His thoughts our thoughts. Instead of allowing the media, an advertising campaign, a company, our family, friends, or others to influence the way we think, we think the way Christ thinks. Doing so shapes our destiny. Why is this so important? Because when we think the way God wants us to think we have a clear understanding of His good, pleasing, and perfect will. The apostle Paul urges us to leave our old ways of thinking behind: "Do not conform any longer to the pattern of this world, but be transformed by the renewing of your mind. Then you will be able to test and approve what God's will is—his good, pleasing and perfect will" (Rom. 12:2).

Everywhere I travel, I ask people, "What is God's will for your life?" Many respond, "You know, I really have no idea." Why is that? Because they still conform to the destructive pattern of this world. They have not been transformed by the renewing of their minds. Their mentality is still clouded. Their minds are bogged down with too many competing ideas, and they can't seem to decipher God's direction.

Most of us face an overload of stimuli. Each day, thousands of images and messages bombard our minds. They come to us through the media, the Internet, politicians, health-care providers, bosses, teachers, friends, and family. Many of these sources demand our attention and insist that they are the experts on life. Our challenge is to filter out the godly from the ungodly, the healthy from the destructive. Unless we change our mind-set, the task of figuring out what we should be doing, where we should be going, or how we're going to get there will be difficult.

YOUR NUMBER-ONE ENEMY

The Bible says, "The mind of sinful man is death, but the mind controlled by the Spirit is life and peace; the sinful mind is hostile to God. It does not submit to God's law, nor can it do so" (Rom. 8:6–7).

The biggest enemy we face is not the person who mistreats us, stands in our way, or spreads lies about us. It's not a misguided religious faith, corrupt financial system, or unjust political ideology. It's not even Satan. The biggest enemy we face is the pattern of destructive thoughts we allow to find a permanent home in our minds. Instead of lifting us up, they tear us down. Instead of inspiring us, they push us toward depression. Instead of guiding us to freedom, they lead us into temptation. Instead of giving us peace and hope, they make us feel anxious and helpless. Although Satan may be our greatest adversary, the thoughts we entertain have an even greater impact on our lives.

What are some of the destructive thoughts you entertain? Are they cruel? Are they negative? Do you place unreasonable expectations on yourself? At one time or another, have you allowed any of the following thoughts to influence you?

Ungodly Thoughts

- *That was so stupid. I should never have said that.*
- *I am such an idiot! Why can't I ever get there on time?*
- *I am not as smart as everyone else. Everyone thinks I am dumb.*
- *My hips are huge. I feel so fat.*
- *My hair is a total disaster.*
- *Could I be any more of a screw-up?*
- *If I lose my job, I'll be living on the streets.*
- *No one really cares.*
- *My heart is racing—I think I'm having a heart attack!*
- *No one loves me.*
- *I really need a fix.*
- *Looking in the mirror, it's obvious that I am getting old.*
- *Life is out of control; I could use a good stiff drink!*
- *If they really knew me, they wouldn't like me.*

- *My best days are behind me.*
- *God must be sick and tired of all my mistakes.*
- *The only reason my husband/wife is still with me is because he/she is fat, too.*

Instead of allowing these destructive thought patterns to influence our behavior, we can choose to implement several powerful habits that will lead to healthy ways of thinking. In Acts 2, the disciples embraced three practices that helped them through difficult times. "They devoted themselves to the apostles' teaching and to the fellowship, to the breaking of bread and to prayer" (Acts 2:42).

As the early church exploded in the New Testament, people everywhere experienced powerful transformations. What guided them through their growth? First, they spent time learning from the apostles' biblical teaching, which renewed their minds. Second, they spent time in fellowship, encouraging one another in the faith. Third, they spent time with God in prayer.

As we apply these three practices to our life, we will discover a roadmap to experiencing the dynamic transformation we seek.

GODLY PRACTICES THAT LEAD TO TRANSFORMATION

1. Spend Time in God's Word

Reading and meditating on God's Word, the first of the godly habits, helps us form a healthy mental picture of who God is, teaches us the difference between godliness and ungodliness, overrides the corrupt patterns that have kept us from experiencing freedom, and initiates powerful changes in our minds. As Scripture tells us, "For everything that was written in the past was written to teach us, so that through endurance and the encouragement of the Scriptures we might have hope" (Rom. 15:4).

In order to renew our minds and experience the power to reinvent ourselves, we need to replace our old ways of thinking with godly ones. The good news is that the apostles' teachings, among many others, are available to us in the Bible. It is an excellent source for godly thought patterns.

Consider the following examples and their scriptural references as an alternative way of thinking to the previous list of ungodly thoughts. Replace each expression on the first list with the godly thoughts on the following pages.

Godly Thoughts

- *That may not have been the best thing to say, but I will make sure I respond more appropriately in the future. God will give me His wisdom.* "If any of you lacks wisdom, he should ask God, who gives generously to all without finding fault, and it will be given to him" (James 1:5).

- *Although I didn't get there on time, my life is a work in progress.* "The one who calls you is faithful and he will do it" (1 Thess. 5:24).

- *I'm not dumb. If I don't understand something, that's fine, as long as I continue to seek the truth.* "For the LORD gives wisdom, and from his mouth come knowledge and understanding" (Prov. 2:6).

- *The Lord wants me to take care of my body, but still loves me just the way I am. He empowers me to resist temptation.* "And lead us not into temptation, but deliver us from the evil one" (Matt. 6:13).

- *Hey, everyone has a bad hair day. Besides, God has seen me at my worst and still loves me.* "O LORD, you have searched me and you know me. You know when I sit and when I rise; you perceive my thoughts from afar. You discern my going out and my lying down; you are familiar with all my ways. Before a word is on my tongue you know it completely, O LORD" (Ps. 139:1–4).

- *God says that I have great worth.* "Keep me as the apple of your eye; hide me in the shadow of your wings" (Ps. 17:8).

- *The Bible says that not one sparrow falls to the ground apart from the will of the Father.* "Therefore I tell you, do not worry about your life, what you will eat or drink; or about your body, what you will wear. Is not life more important than food, and the body more important than clothes? Look at the birds of the air; they do not sow or reap or store away in barns, and yet your heavenly Father feeds them. Are you not much more valuable than they?" (Matt. 6:25–26).

- *God cares. I have friends and family who care.* "You hem me in—behind and before; you have laid your hand upon me. Such knowledge is too wonderful for me, too lofty for me to attain" (Ps. 139:5–6).

- *Most people are afraid of things that never happen. The Lord will help me in my hour of anxiousness.* "Do not be anxious about anything, but in everything, by prayer and petition, with thanksgiving, present your requests to God" (Phil. 4:6).

- *God loves me.* "However, the LORD your God…turned the curse into a blessing for you, because the LORD your God loves you" (Deut. 23:5).

- *God sees me as His child.* "You are all sons of God through faith in Christ Jesus" (Gal. 3:26).

- *God has everything under control, and He said He would take care of my needs.* "And we know that in all things God works for the good of those who love him, who have been called according to his purpose" (Rom. 8:28).

- *People who know me care about me.* "Dear friends, since God so loved us, we also ought to love one another" (1 John 4:11).

- *Commitment and love go far beyond looks. Besides, with God, all things are possible. I can work diligently to change any aspect of my life.* "Jesus looked at them and said, 'With man this is impossible, but not with God; all things are possible with God'" (Mark 10:27).

- *God says that as long as I obey and keep His commandments, I will continue to walk in His blessings.* "If you fully obey the LORD your God and carefully follow all his commands I give you today, the LORD your God will set you high above all the nations on earth. All these blessings will come upon you and accompany you if you obey the LORD your God" (Deut. 28:1–2).

- *God's mercy and forgiveness are infinite.* "Give thanks to the Lord of lords: His love endures forever. To him who alone does great wonders, His love endures forever" (Ps. 136:3–4).
- *God wants me to have a healthy, God-fearing marriage. Our commitment is much deeper than physical appearance.* "Charm is deceptive, and beauty is fleeting; but a woman who fears the LORD is to be praised" (Prov. 31:30).

When we stand back and look at the two lists outlined previously, the contrast is like night and day. One represents what Satan wants you to think. The other represents what God wants you to think. There is, in essence, a war between two kingdoms.

Paul understood that the war is waged not in a physical place but in our minds. The kingdom of God and the kingdom of Satan wage war twenty-four hours a day, seven days a week, over the thoughts in our minds.

If we allow ungodly thoughts to run rampant, we will live destructive lives plagued by the patterns that keep us in bondage. If we become transformed by the renewing of our minds, then we will live godly and blessed lives, and the presence of the kingdom of God will be evident in us. Again, who we are and what we do is determined by the way we think. So how do we become transformed by the renewing of our minds?

We become godly in our thinking by making every thought obedient to Christ. "The weapons we fight with are not the weapons of the world. On the contrary, they have divine power to demolish strongholds. We demolish arguments and every pretension that sets itself up against the knowledge of God, and we take captive every thought to make it obedient to Christ" (2 Cor. 10:4–5). We judge every thought against what the Word defines as godly and acceptable. This is why reading and meditating on the Scripture is imperative—because it helps us form new and godly thoughts.

∽◈∾

We loaded up our semis with forty tons of crusade gear and made the five-hour trip to one of the most remote communities in the country. In order to save some driving time, we decided to cross over to the peninsula on a ferry. As we approached the shore, a torrential downpour hit the town with a vengeance. It dumped over three inches of rain in an hour-and-a-half.

By the time we arrived at the crusade site, the mud was six inches deep. Our well-trained team, along with fifty volunteers from local churches, endured the ninety-degree temperature and began to work. Within six hours, the stage, sound, lighting, and chairs were set up.

Situated behind our platform was one of the most powerful radio stations in the northern province of the country. Its antenna, over fifteen stories tall, was the background for what would be a memorable four-day event. At 7:00 p.m., the citywide outreach was under way with three thousand people in attendance.

We had a wonderful musical group traveling with us. The seventy-thousand watts of power from our sound system helped to carry their music for several city blocks. Little did I know that a problem was brewing that would almost derail my ability to reach someone special.

In between each song, we noticed the faint sound of music coming through our speakers. At first, I thought it was one of the sound engineers playing with the CD player. If that were the case, we could have easily solved the problem. No such luck. Finally, one of our coordinators discovered the source of the intrusive music—the radio station right behind our platform! At 7:00 p.m., the station boosted its signal in order to reach a greater audience. Our amplifiers picked up their frequency and pushed it through the speakers.

As long as the band was playing, no one could hear it. But eventually I would pick up the microphone and be left to fend for myself. Sure enough, as soon as I started to preach, an old classic rock song, "Hotel California," hit the airwaves. The popular tune was an allegory about being trapped in hell. Without hesitation, I signaled to the keyboardist to come back to the stage and play something—anything. As soon as he turned on his Yamaha, he began playing "Lord, I Give You My Heart."

Hearing two songs simultaneously was terribly distracting. Several of the ushers looked as if they had swallowed a lemon peel. Perhaps because our talented keyboard player couldn't handle the dissonance, he eventually ceased to play the worship song and joined in the melody of "Hotel California."

For a moment, I thought I was going insane.

I became so frustrated and angry over the unwanted music that my old ways of thinking distracted me from my true mission. Thank God, no storm lasts forever, not even the perfect storm. Finally, one of our technicians ran to the station and explained what was happening. They kindly made the adjustments, and within several minutes the problem was resolved. Unfortunately, I was still flustered, to the point that I couldn't think straight.

That's when Victoria appeared at the back of the crowd. The pretty teenage girl had been walking down the street and heard a message mixed with a colorful assortment of music. She paused for a few moments before coming in. I have no idea what I said that night, but something resonated with her. When I gave the invitation for people to begin a relationship with God, she raised her hand and came forward.

I remember looking down from the five-foot stage and seeing her standing all by herself. She looked into my eyes as the tears streamed down her face. Up until that moment, I was a bit out of touch, still trying to get over the music fiasco. When I saw her expression, everything changed. One of our crusade workers was standing behind her. I signaled her to approach Victoria and find out if there was something wrong. Indeed, there was.

She began to converse with the worker, who then asked me to talk to her. When I came off the platform, the mud nearly sucked the shoes off my feet. I found a solid place to stand, and that's when Victoria began to tell me her story.

She said, "Jason, I came here because you said that Christ could set the captive free. He could break any chains and give me the freedom I've only dreamed of having. Well, I have been living in chains for ten years. I want to know if what you said is really true. Can Jesus set me free?"

"Of course," I responded. "What do you need to be set free from?"

Victoria said, "Ten years ago, I was raped repeatedly by a relative. Since that horrific time in my life, I am tormented every time I go to bed. Early every morning my closet doors suddenly open, and different objects start to levitate. On several occasions, my bed sheets have floated above my body. No matter how hard I try, I can't seem to stop the voices in my head telling me to commit suicide. So let me ask you again, do you really believe that Christ can set me free?"

Although deep down inside my heart was hurting for this young lady, I did my best to maintain my composure. I immediately replied, "Absolutely."

For more than ten years, the enemy had forged patterns of self-destruction in her mind. The spiritual attacks were overwhelming, and the pressure was much more than anyone should ever have to endure. Many of the things Victoria thought about herself had to be relearned. The habits had to be erased and new ones had to be established. That is precisely what we set out to do.

I asked two of our female counselors to assist me in praying for Victoria. Each one placed a hand on one of her shoulders, and we began to pray. I asked the Lord to set her free and place His hand on her life. I prayed that He would break her chains and renew her mind. She simply covered her eyes and wailed. Despite ten years of accumulated pain, the Lord had come to meet her on a humble lot at the far end of the country to help her experience true freedom. After praying, I instructed one of the counselors to embrace Victoria until she no longer needed someone to hold her.

As the first night came to a close, the counselor sat down with Victoria and urged her to put into practice several transforming principles. She gave her a list of Scriptures to read each day to help her renew her confused mind. She strongly urged her to find a church. She stressed the importance of spending time every day with the Lord in prayer.

Each night of the campaign, Victoria came and listened. During the last night, she approached the platform and motioned to me that she wanted to speak with me. She said, "Ever since we prayed, I have had no trouble sleeping. I have been reading those Scripture verses every day, and whenever I feel anxious, I read them again. I no longer hear those diabolic voices of suicide in my head. There haven't been any more strange early morning occurrences!"

"That's wonderful!" I said.

"But," she said, "I am afraid that everything will go back to the way it was. Will you pray one more time? Please pray that the transformation I've experienced will stay with me for good."

Overwhelmed with compassion, I said, "Victoria, I would be honored." We prayed that the Lord would finish the work that He began in her. It's a promise that we can all count on. God finishes the work He begins in us (Phil. 1:6).

When we finished praying, I asked her, "Would you like one of our counselors to walk you home?"

"No, thank you," she said. "Actually, I am headed to the bus stop to travel back home."

"Home?" I asked. "Who brought you to this event?"

"No one," she replied. "I'm not from here. I live on the other side of the country."

"How did you discover this event?" I asked.

She said, "I'm here on vacation. I was walking down the street and someone handed me this flyer." She pulled out a crumpled piece of paper. "And I saw the words 'There is hope in Jesus.' I knew I needed help. I needed the power to change. I needed someone to set me free. That's how I wound up here."

One of our counselors escorted Victoria to the bus stop and watched her climb aboard. Tucked under her arm was a New Testament she had received from us along with the list of Bible verses that helped her become transformed by the renewing of her mind.

2. Spend Time in Fellowship

The second godly habit is meeting regularly with others who have the same spiritual convictions we do. Participating in corporate worship is both biblical and necessary for our growth. The Bible says, "Let us not give up meeting together, as some are in the habit of doing, but let us encourage one another—and all the more as you see the Day approaching" (Heb. 10:25). The writer of Hebrews understood the importance of corporate worship for the spiritual development of the believer. That is why he expressed his concern that many people were no longer meeting on a regular basis. Today, we seem to be facing a similar issue.

In 1990, I started out in ministry as an itinerant missionary speaker in churches across the country. Since that time, I have noticed a downward trend in church attendance. By that, I mean less people are in church on a weekly basis, and churches have fewer services each week, specifically on Sunday night.[1] By all indications, this trend is not expected to reverse itself in the near future.[2]

Why are fewer people attending worship services each week? The biggest reason seems to be lack of interest. When I ask people why they do not attend church on a given Sunday, many say they don't feel like they get anything out of the experience. They don't feel as though their needs are being met. For them, it's not worth the effort.

Another reason may be that people's schedules are more complicated than ever. Much of their work spills over into Sunday. Businesses are open seven days a week with longer hours each day. People are constantly trying to play catch up, and Sunday is the one day that offers the flexibility to regain lost ground. And some people believe that going to church takes away the only time they have to spend with their family.

What relevance does this trend have to our ability to experience God's power to reinvent ourselves? Odds are that over time we will be tempted to reduce our involvement in the local church. This is potentially dangerous for our spiritual health and the spiritual health of our families. Inevitably, a reduction in church attendance leads to less interest in godly things.

When there is less interest in godly things, patterns of destruction quickly settle in. Then we find ourselves back at the beginning of the process, needing help and crying out for freedom from the bondage that keeps us from moving forward.

I am not saying that church attendance is an end in itself. But it is a vital part of the process of experiencing true freedom. It's a godly habit, one that the Lord says should be practiced weekly. "Remember the Sabbath day by keeping it holy" (Exod. 20:8). Being in church gives us the opportunity to experience God's presence and to be surrounded by others who will inspire and build us up spiritually. It has immeasurable benefits for our lives.

Faithfully attending church helps us stay connected to other people who share our faith, where there is protection and blessing. When we disassociate ourselves from others, we run the risk of getting off track for transformation. "Now you are the body of Christ, and each one of you is a part of it" (1 Cor. 12:27).

Participating in an accountability group is not the same as church attendance. Attending church incorporates us into a larger group of believers. Accountability groups are formed for the members of that particular group. I will discuss in greater depth the function of a group of trusted friends in chapter 6.

So what are some of the benefits of meeting on a

weekly basis with other believers? First, being in church on a regular basis is a biblical mandate and contributes to our spiritual health. By gathering together, we learn to worship, pray, and study the Scriptures guided by those who are more mature in the Lord (Heb. 13:17). This prevents us from moving away from the foundation of sound doctrine. It also keeps us from mystical interpretations of Scripture and from basing our theology solely on our own unique experience.

Second, being in church on a regular basis has a positive impact on our ability to stay physically and emotionally healthy. Claudia Wallis wrote a highly insightful article that pointed to studies that indicated that people who attend church have lower blood pressure, are more likely to recover after surgery, are less likely to develop coronary artery disease, and are less likely to become depressed.[3] The suicide rate among nonchurchgoers is four times higher than among those who regularly attend church. In light of these findings, church attendance may actually save our lives.

Third, in a healthy church, people are challenged to become part of a mission that is greater than their own personal agenda. The core of the church's mission is reaching out to those who need the Good News, the proclamation of the gospel. In order to complete such an overwhelming task, we need to be part of a large team of believers. The task of sharing the gospel with a world that desperately needs God is a universal mandate for all believers, and it demands that we work together (Mark 16:15–16).

Further, part of the mission of the church is to help people with their basic physical needs. For that reason, churches, both Protestant and Catholic, build hospitals, universities, food banks, orphanages, and schools around the world. Being associated with a local group of believers helps us fulfill this part of the mission. Being connected to a local body of believers greatly increases our effectiveness to reach the world spiritually and physically.

In light of these three powerful benefits, consider making your involvement in a local church a priority. Doing so will create one of the three godly habits that will help you break the patterns that have kept you from moving in the direction God wants you to go.

The heart of the church. Many times we think of church as a physical place with a steeple, pews, organ, pulpit, and a choir loft. Instead of defining church as a physical place where people meet, I would like to give you another image. The church is a group of people who gather regularly to worship, pray, and study the Bible. One of its primary functions is to give spiritual guidance so those who attend can negotiate their way through life. That's what a healthy body of Christians does. They take care of each other. Recently, a friend of mine related a story that wonderfully illustrates this.

Kevin, a young boy, had been abused, neglected, and abandoned by his father. A foster child, he was filled with fears and had difficulty trusting people. One day, he received an invitation to go to a camp where kids with similar backgrounds could enjoy a fun-filled week at a lake. There, counselors and leaders poured their hearts into each child for five days. Their goal was to build up the campers' confidence and inspire them to do something they never would have dreamed of doing before.

At this particular camp, fishing was a favorite activity. There was a staffer named Mark who taught the children how to fish off a dock. Mark knew that such an accomplishment would have a positive impact on the campers.

Young Kevin not only needed a positive experience, he needed a miracle. There was a problem, though. Kevin was deathly afraid of the water. On his top ten list of fears, being close to the lake was number one. So after the kids unpacked their suitcases, his counselor began to look for a creative way for Kevin to experience the joy of catching a fish.

No matter what idea he came up with, Kevin

declined. Then the counselor suggested that Kevin could dress up in a special costume. He handed him a life jacket and asked if he would like to put it on. Kevin liked the idea, since many of the other campers wore other types of costumes. That day, as he wore the life jacket, the counselors told him how great he looked. The other kids admired his official safety gear. He wore it to breakfast, lunch, and dinner. It became his uniform.

The second day, the counselor convinced Kevin to walk down by the lake. "Hey, while we are here, why don't we take a few minutes and build a sandcastle here on the shore?" the counselor asked. Kevin was reluctant, but the counselor pointed out that Kevin already had his life jacket on. So Kevin plopped down and began forming different images in the sand. Over the course of several days, his confidence grew.

As Kevin worked on his sand creation, he noticed the other kids were not afraid of the water. In fact, they were laughing and enjoying themselves. Some of them were catching fish. So toward the end of the third day, his counselor asked him if he wanted to go out onto the dock and meet Mark. "No, thank you," he replied.

"Come on. It will be fun. We'll just walk out on the dock and meet the great fisherman. Besides, Kevin, you already have your life jacket on," the counselor said.

Kevin finally agreed. He and his counselor slowly walked onto the dock. With each step he took, his heart raced faster and faster. Although he was heading out to meet the camp's coolest guy, he was inching closer to his greatest fear. As they approached, Mark's face lit up. "Hello, Kevin!" he said. "I am so glad you joined us today! You look like such a big boy in that life jacket! Here, I have something for you." Reaching down, Mark grabbed a fishing pole and placed it in Kevin's hands. Even though the boy did not act excited, all could see in his eyes the desire to hold that fishing pole.

"Hey, since you're here, why don't we put some bait on that hook?" Mark said. He then reached into a jar, removed some bait, and placed it on the hook. Kevin stood there stiffly. After all, he had never been so close to something so terrifying.

Trying to be positive, Mark said, "Tell you what. Let me show you how to cast your line. Nothing can happen to you while I show you how to cast your line out in the lake. This is how you do it." He pushed the button on the reel, pulled the pole back over his shoulder, and whipped it in the direction of the lake. The hook and bait hurled through the air.

How cool is that? Kevin thought.

After several casts, Mark turned to the boy and asked him if he wanted to give it a try. Kevin warmed to the idea and grabbed the pole. They carefully walked up to the edge of the dock. Kevin was now standing within twelve inches of the water. This was momentous for him.

Imitating Mark, Kevin pressed the button on the reel, whipped the pole back over his right shoulder, and launched his fishing line with all of his might. Unfortunately, he cast with such force that he went flying head first into the water. His worst nightmare became a reality.

The eyes of Mark, the counselor, and other campers were as big as saucers as they watched the scene unfold. Almost as quickly as Kevin hit the water, the counselor jumped in after him. Mark dove onto his belly on the dock and as soon as Kevin bobbed back to the surface, he grabbed his life jacket and pulled him out of the water.

Just a few seconds after his mighty cast, Kevin stood on the dock dripping wet. As he spit out the water he had taken in, both the counselor and Mark noticed something interesting. Kevin was still gripping the fishing pole. Through it all, he never let go.

Suddenly, the tip of the pole began moving downward sporadically. Where the bait used to be, a fish now wiggled on the end of Kevin's line.

A look of amazement came over Kevin's face. He had caught a fish! He felt powerful facing his greatest fear and overcoming it. Kevin spent the remainder of his time at camp with his feet dangling off the edge of the dock, fishing next to a friendly fellow fisherman named Mark.

There was no way Kevin could have made that breakthrough had it not been for the caring Christian people who took him by the hand and walked him through the process. That is precisely what a healthy church does. A group of godly people of like faith can help guide us through the temptations, fears, and challenges we face and help us grow in our relationship with God. This is the heart of what it means to be a church.

Being in church is a vital habit that enables us to get past the things that hold us back. Attending church on a regular basis has spiritual and physical benefits, and it ties us to a corporate mission that allows us to touch the world (Matt. 28:19–20).

The first two godly habits we've studied thus far help us renew our minds and grow with other believers. The third habit we will now discuss is one of the most important godly habits we can develop.

3. Spend Time with God in Prayer

Spending time with God in prayer changes things, both externally and internally. Let's look first at an example of how prayer can change external circumstances.

Prayer changes the external. One day a wealthy woman and her husband invited a prophet named Elisha into their home for a meal. After that, when he traveled through that region, he stayed with the family. Recognizing that Elisha was a holy man, the couple decided to make a room on the top floor of their home for him.

As he grew to know the family, Elisha had compassion on the woman, because she had no children and her husband was old. So one day, Elisha said to her, "About this time next year, you will hold a son in your arms." But the woman felt overwhelmed. She didn't want to be filled with false hopes. "No, my lord," she objected. "Don't mislead your servant, O man of God!" (2 Kings 4:16).

But within a few short months, the woman became pregnant and gave birth to a son. As the boy grew older, he went with his father to work in the fields. One day, he suddenly experienced a severe pain in his head. The father told one of the workers to carry the boy back to his mother. So the servant did what he was told. The boy sat on his mother's lap, and at the noon hour, he died.

With a broken heart, the woman picked up her dead son and carried him upstairs to the room they had prepared for Elisha. She gently laid the boy on the bed, shut the door, and left. She then saddled up a donkey and rode off to find Elisha.

When she finally reached Elisha, she grabbed hold of his feet and said, "Did I ask you for a son, my lord?...Didn't I tell you, 'Don't raise my hopes'?" (2 Kings 4:28). Immediately, Elisha turned to his servant and said, "Tuck your cloak into your belt, take my staff in your hand and run. If you meet anyone, do not greet him, and if anyone greets you, do not answer. Lay my staff on the boy's face" (v. 29).

The woman was determined not to leave Elisha's side. He had delivered a wonderful promise to her. That promise became a reality, and in one afternoon, it was taken from her. She said to him, "As surely as the LORD lives and as you live, I will not leave you" (v. 30). So Elisha did not stay behind. Instead, he accompanied her back to her house.

In the meantime, Gehazi did exactly what Elisha told him to do. He quickly ran ahead to the house without speaking to anyone along the way. When he arrived, he rushed to the upper room and laid Elisha's staff on the boy's face. But there was no response.

After a short time, he ran back to meet Elisha along the way and told him, "The boy has not awakened" (v. 31). The three of them continued to the house, and when they went upstairs, Elisha saw the boy lying dead on the bed in the room the couple had made for him. No one said a word. Elisha entered the room alone, turned, and shut the door. Lifting his eyes toward heaven, he prayed to the Lord.

Then he did something extraordinary. He climbed onto the bed and stretched himself out over the child, lying on top of him, matching hands to hands, eyes to eyes, mouth to mouth. Time passed and eventually the boy's body started to grow warm.

Elisha got up and began to pace back and forth. Then the prophet returned to the bed and stretched out over the boy again. Suddenly, the child sneezed seven times, opened his eyes, and looked around. Elisha opened the door and instructed Gehazi to call the boy's mother. When she entered the room, Elisha handed her the child.

Prayer changes the external. It changes our circumstances, conditions, and surroundings. Prayer changes things that seem unchangeable, things that are beyond our control.

Among the many lessons we can learn from Elisha's experience, two in particular will help us in our journey to move beyond the things that hold us back. First, *there is no substitute for prayer*. When Elisha sent his servant with his staff to minister to the needs of a family in crisis, there was no response. It was only when Elisha prayed that the hand of God began to move.

God wants to hear our hearts. The practice of spending time with the Lord is something we must work to build. And when we build a healthy prayer life, God begins to move in our lives.

Second, *even when we face impossible odds, prayer changes things*. You learn that God comes through even when things look bleak. In your darkest hour, God responds when you speak from your heart. He listens to your petitions and understands your needs.

For example, we have the story of Hannah, who longed for a child but couldn't conceive:

In bitterness of soul Hannah wept much and prayed to the LORD. And she made a vow, saying, "O LORD Almighty, if you will only look upon your servant's misery and remember me, and not forget your servant but give her a son, then I will give him to the LORD for all the days of his life, and no razor will ever be used on his head."...So in the course of time Hannah conceived and gave birth to a son. She named him Samuel, saying, "Because I asked the LORD for him." (1 Samuel 1:10–11, 20)

When, like Hannah, your back is to the wall, call out to the Lord. He will hear you. If you feel that all hope is lost and there's no way out, ask the Lord to intervene. When you do, believe God will act, and He will!

God responds to prayer, even when we least expect it. The phone rang at 7:30 a.m. "Jason, I've got some good news," my supervisor said. "Your dreams of holding an evangelistic campaign are about to come true. A large church is sending a construction team and a medical team to work during the day. They also want to sponsor an evangelistic outreach at night. Can you coordinate it and be the translator for their pastor?" To say that I was excited is an understatement.

The town in which we were to hold the outreach was a small, marginalized community on the outskirts of San Jose, Costa Rica. I found the ideal lot and asked a good friend, Danilo Montero, to lead worship. Our team arranged the electrical hookups, installed the light towers, and handed out tens of thousands of flyers. I drove down to the company that rented the biggest moveable stage in the nation. It was the same one used by the president of the country during his run for office.

Two days later, the large semi truck dropped off the forty-foot trailer that converted into a platform. One of its walls was permanent. The other lowered ninety degrees and became the stage. However, when we tried to lower it, one of the hinges broke, and the entire stage smashed to the ground. I couldn't believe my eyes. *This is the president's stage*, I thought. *And now it looks like a crushed tin can.* Without hesitation, we pulled a number of team members off the construction site and put them to work on welding the stage back together. Finally it was fixed.

During the day, volunteers at the medical clinic had attended to hundreds of people in the community. That night, the evangelistic outreach got under way. At the close of the first night, we gave an altar call for people who had needs. Half the crowd came forward. In spite of my exhaustion and the feeling that I was in over my head, I asked God for the strength to pray for each one individually.

The first person who came forward for prayer was Paula, a young girl escorted by her grandmother. The elderly lady asked me, "Would you please pray for my granddaughter?" I said, "Sure" and got down on one knee to learn more about her particular need. I said, "Would you like us to pray for you?" The child's only response was a rapid head nod. The tears streaming down her face led me to believe that she was frightened about something.

The grandmother said, "Last week, I noticed that she was walking with a slight inclination to her left. So I took her to the clinic earlier today, and the x-rays indicated that she was missing three ribs on her left side. The doctors said they need to operate, but we don't have the money. We need a miracle. I believe God can heal her, but the doctors warned us that if we don't operate, she's going to be an invalid." The news had devastated the elderly woman.

I looked into Paula's tear-filled eyes and asked, "Honey, do you believe God can heal you?" She nodded in agreement. I said, "Okay, we're going to pray for you." We prayed for her, and after two minutes, we moved on to the other 299 people who were patiently waiting.

At the end of that night I felt a tug on my jacket. It was Paula. She looked up at me and said, "I believe the Lord has healed me." I was skeptical and said, "Well, we probably should have a doctor take a look at that."

Paula grabbed my hand and pointed to someone

with her other hand. She said, "That man is a doctor." So I walked over to him and said, "Excuse me, but this young lady went into a clinic earlier this morning." Before I could finish my sentence, his face lit up. "Yes, I examined her this morning," he said. "She is missing three ribs on her left side. I am afraid she has curvature of the spine. If we don't operate on her, she will be an invalid."

I explained all that had happened, how we prayed for her, and what she said to me after the service. "She says that the Lord has healed her," I told the doctor.

He responded, "Well, I can examine her right now. If she is healed, it will be obvious." So he asked her to bend at the waist and lifted up her shirt. He gently moved his fingers starting at the top of the spine and looked for any obvious holes. Then he counted by twos from the bottom of her neck to the lower part of her back. He looked at me with both eyebrows lifted. He said, "The girl who came into the clinic this morning was definitely missing ribs. The little girl standing in front of us has a perfect spine." The next day, Paula and her grandmother went back to the clinic where the doctor verified what had happened.

Prayer changes external circumstances. It changes people and impacts those around us. Its impact is immeasurable. During one particularly difficult and trying time, God demonstrated to me that He indeed answers prayer.

Ten years had passed since Paula's healing, and I was standing in the second largest stadium in Central America. It was the first night of the final crusade we held in 2004. The rains had pounded the city and deterred thousands of people from coming to the outreach. Needless to say, I was discouraged. Approximately six thousand people were in attendance. But in a stadium that seats twenty-seven thousand, the crowd seemed sparse. I closed the message that night with a final illustration and told the story of Paula.

When I reached the conclusion and shared the words of the doctor, the crowd erupted into applause. Suddenly I noticed someone walking from the first row to the side of the stage. She motioned to the stage manager who then escorted the young woman to me. Although at first I didn't recognize her, when she got closer, I couldn't believe my eyes. It was Paula! Of all people, the first person I prayed for in a campaign was standing before me over a decade later. I cried with joy.

Now she was a fully grown woman. By every definition, she was normal, free from any disability, abnormality, or deformity. God sent her, once again, during a time when I needed a shot in the arm. I was reminded that prayer really does change the external.

When we pray, God responds. His mighty hand begins to work, and we can count on the promise that He always hears us and responds. Although His response sometimes is different than what we might expect, nevertheless God will answer.

We have discovered the dynamic impact that prayer has on our external circumstances. Now we will discover how prayer changes us internally, the way we think, feel, and perceive the world.

Prayer changes the internal. Peter is one of the most prominent and well-known disciples in the Bible. Yet, from the time he became a follower of Jesus to the time after the Resurrection that he tried to convince Christ that he loved Him, over and over again Peter displayed a lack of confidence. Perhaps that is why so many people identify with him. In Matthew 14, Peter got out of a boat, walked on water, and within seconds started to sink. In Mark 8, Jesus rebuked him and referred to him as Satan. In Matthew 26, Peter swore that he would never deny Christ, only to fall desperately short before the rooster crowed a third time. In Mark 14, he fell asleep in the garden when the Lord specifically told him to stay awake and pray for just an hour. In Luke 5, when Peter saw the miraculous catch of fish, he fell to his knees and said, "Go away from me, Lord; I am a sinful man!" (v. 8). Finally in

John 21, Jesus had to ask Peter three times whether or not he loved Him.

Throughout the four Gospels, the picture we have of Peter is that of an inconsistent disciple who knows the truth but has difficulty doing what he knows is right. Something begins to happen, though, as we open the book of Acts. A revolution starts to take place in Peter's heart.

After Jesus was taken up into heaven, 120 disciples assembled together to pray continually. Peter was the first preacher to emerge from that group. He encouraged the disciples every day. He taught them with a newfound authority and led them through the process of selecting an apostle to replace Judas.

After days of prayer, the morning of Pentecost came. It was one of the most important days recorded in the New Testament. Why? Because it changed the world forever. The disciples were together when suddenly a strong wind began to blow and filled the entire place where they were sitting. Fiery images appeared over their heads that seemed to have the form of tongues. The images separated and rested on those who were present. Each person, male and female, was filled with the Holy Spirit and began to speak in other tongues as the Spirit gave them the ability to do so.

There was some confusion among those who were

outside the building where the disciples were gathered. As they heard the different languages, many of them asked each other what the strange phenomena was. Still others began to make fun of the disciples, accusing them of having too much wine with breakfast. While they were discussing the issue, one disciple stood to his feet, raised his voice, and began to address the crowd. He communicated one of the greatest messages recorded in church history. It clearly explained God's purpose for sending Jesus and the decision that people should make as a result of hearing the message. That day, three thousand people became followers of Christ. Who was the preacher? Peter.

Subsequently, in Acts 3, both Peter and John headed to the temple and met a crippled man who was begging for money. Instead of looking the opposite way, Peter challenged him. He walked over and said, "Silver or gold I do not have, but what I have I give you. In the name of Jesus Christ of Nazareth, walk" (Acts 3:6). Then he bent down and helped the beggar to his feet. The man was instantly healed!

Peter's reputation as a man filled with the power of God grew to the extent that "people brought the sick into the streets and laid them on beds and mats so that at least Peter's shadow might fall on some of them as he passed by" (Acts 5:15).

Peter was no longer an inconsistent, half-disciplined man who couldn't keep his focus. The turning point for him came as he spent time in prayer leading up to and culminating with the day of Pentecost. He was transformed by the power of God through a diligent prayer life.

When we spend time talking with God, something in us begins to change. We become more like Him. We take on His character. We develop His love for others. We become concerned about people. We carry His burden for the poor. We gain a heart of compassion for others. Praying not only connects us with a God who touches our lives in times of need, but it also helps center our off-centered lives. No matter who you are or what your past is, prayer will make a definitive difference in your life. It's true that prayer changes people. And the most important person prayer changes is you.

The power of God in a Jacuzzi. In the fall of 1981, I was just beginning my spiritual journey. From a back row seat in my high school English class, I heard another student mention that he liked a contemporary Christian artist named Keith Green. I had one of Green's albums, so I asked the student if he was a Christian. He replied, "Why, yes, I am."

As class ended, we conversed for about ten minutes.

He then asked if I wanted to go over to his house that afternoon to shoot a few games of pool. That sounded great, especially since the only billiard table I had seen was in a bar, and as a minor, I wasn't allowed to play.

I will never forget walking into his three-thousand-square-foot, three-level house. It had a gymnasium, recreation room, an indoor spa, and Jacuzzi. The pool table could be converted into a ping-pong table. It was everything a teenager could want.

After playing a couple of games of pool, we got in the Jacuzzi and started to talk about how we met Christ. He confessed to me that earlier in his life, he needed help. So a pastor reached out and taught him the importance of prayer and reading the Bible. The pastor guided him in a disciplined spiritual workout to remove the destructive patterns he had developed. Then he started implementing new habits so that he would not fall back into his old ways. Six months later, we were sitting in his hot tub.

After telling me about how God helped him through those tough times, he said, "You know, many students just like us need God's help. Why don't we spend a few minutes and pray for our high school?"

I confess to you, friend, that I had never prayed in public before. For that matter, I had never prayed out loud. So you can imagine my reaction. Within seconds, I could feel my blood pressure shooting up. I thought, *How do you pray out loud in a way that sounds spiritual?* Then, another voice in my head took over, the one that comes from God's Word. The Bible verses that I read from the time I had the encounter in that church soon came to mind. *God wants us to pray,* I thought. *God wants to hear from us. He wants to hear me pray.*

"Let's go for it," I said. "But you go first!"

My friend prayed with conviction and enthusiasm, raising his voice and crying out to God. He expressed impressive and powerful words that I know pleased the Lord. He asked God to rescue those who were lost, suffering, lonely, and alienated. He asked God to help people discover the truth and to bring about a spiritual revolution in our high school. When he finished his prayer, he looked at me and nodded to indicate that it was now my turn.

I waited for a moment, took a deep breath, and said, "Yeah! What he just said!"

I discovered one important lesson through that experience. As long as our hearts are sincere, just about any prayer is good enough. In the months that followed, I continued to develop a prayer life. Each day, I dedicated time to talk with God. Whether I was walking to the bus stop or sitting in my room, I talked to Him as I would to my best friend. Those times of prayer had a profound impact on my life. As a result, God began to change my character. The temptations I faced were difficult and at times overwhelming, but after spending time in prayer, they became manageable. God helped me replace many of the destructive patterns with one that made a significant difference. Prayer had an *internal* impact on my life. Because of prayer, I am a completely different person.

One of the greatest things you can do to initiate change in your life is pray. You can develop the habit of spending time with God. Start today. Doing so will revolutionize your life.

When my family and I lived in Central America, we had a yard that was filled with weeds. I called the gardener, and about once a month he would remove them. Within three weeks, they were back. Finally, I asked him why it was so difficult to have a weed-free yard. His response was surprising. "The birds," he said. "They believe it's their job to spread the seed. Unless you can get rid of all the birds, you'll just have to keep cleaning out the weeds."

The same is true regarding the buildup of destructive patterns in our lives. Many things influence the way we think. Some are helpful. Some are not. Being

144

transformed by renewing our minds is like the cleaning process of a gardener. Every so often, we have to clean out the accumulation of weeds. We do that by reading God's Word, getting together with other believers, and spending time in prayer.

As we end this chapter, reflect upon the three godly habits that lead to transformation and ask yourself the following questions:

Have I been reading my Bible? If not, perhaps you should start.

Do I regularly attend a church or weekly meeting? Maybe it's time to find a church where you and your family will be encouraged in your faith.

Do I spend sufficient time with the Lord in prayer? He loves you and desires to spend time with you each day.

You are important to God, and He can help you get past the things that hold you back if you give Him a chance. There is no one who thinks as highly of you as the Lord. You are always on His mind. These three habits will empower you to reinvent yourself. They can be the start of an amazing life filled with meaning and significance.

It is appropriate that we conclude this chapter with

a short prayer. Again, I leave this with you in case you appreciate a guide. Before I wrote out this prayer for you, I prayed that you would sense God's presence as you talked with Him.

Lord, once again, I recognize that You are the source of life. I ask You to help me implement new and godly habits. Help me to be transformed by the renewing of my mind. Show me new insights in Your Word so that I can understand it better. Lead me to a church or regular meeting and help me to become involved so that I can learn more about You. I want to establish meaningful relationships that will help me grow. And help me move away from those relationships that are destructive and harmful. I also ask You to help me pray. Help me to always turn to You in my time of need, opening the lines of communication so that I do not sink into depression or loneliness. Finally, I ask You to remove me from temptation. Deliver me from those things that are enticing and harmful. I ask these things in Christ's name. Amen.

CHAPTER 5

Choose to Forgive

IT WAS A WARM summer night in Southern California. The humidity was low, twilight was still visible, and my excitement was high. My mom and I were heading to the drug store to buy some ice cream. For a six-year-old, there was nothing better after a hot summer day.

I remember driving into the parking lot in the west end of the San Fernando Valley. My mom parked her 1969 Volkswagen Bug and started to dig into her hippie-style leather purse, scrounging around for thirty cents. In those days that was what it cost for two double ice cream cones. After finding a quarter and a nickel, she looked at me and said, "Now remember, I want a double cone with pistachio and coffee ice cream."

She handed me the two coins and sent me on my

way. I must have repeated the combination of flavors at least twenty times before I reached the store entrance. I was determined to show her that I could do it by myself. *I am a big boy*, I thought.

The clerk leaned over the top of the refrigerated bin and said, "May I help you?"

I said, "Yeah, I'll take one cone with rocky road and mint 'n' chip. And I'll take another cone with pistachio and coffee."

"Will that be all?" he asked.

"That will be all," I confidently replied.

I waited patiently for both ice cream cones. The tension was building. I knew that I had to pay and hurry back to the car before the ice cream began to melt. I handed the clerk the money, and he handed me the two cones. I turned and stepped onto the mat that opened the automatic door and headed to the parking lot.

I didn't want to wait until I reached the car to give my cone a try. So I raised my ice cream to my mouth and nibbled off a small portion of the frosty mint 'n' chip. How refreshing. I continued to walk and took another small bite. *This is living,* I thought. Unfortunately, it is hard to do three things at once—especially when they include walking, eating ice cream, and holding your mother's cone in an upright position.

As I took another bite, I failed to notice that my

mom's cone was leaning at a forty-five-degree angle. When I finally realized what was happening, the Leaning Tower of Pisa had begun to fall. The ice cream dropped from the cone in slow motion, toppling end over end, until finally it splattered right smack in the middle of a parking spot.

To a little boy, ice cream on the ground is just as good as ice cream on the cone. So I bent down, scraped up the ice cream, slapped it back on the cone, and headed to the car. This time, I thought it would be best not to take any more bites until I reached the car.

My mom looked so excited to see her son serving her a sugar cone with her favorite flavors towering high above. "You did it," she said. I beamed with pride and jumped in the back seat.

I watched her in the rearview mirror as she started in on her cone. After about the third lick, she pulled something off of her tongue. Scrunching her eyebrows downward, she mumbled to herself, "What is this? Is this glass?"

After pulling it off of her tongue, she quietly wiped it on a napkin. The next lick, she frowned again and said, "There is a hair in my mouth . . . and this ice cream tastes like motor oil." She angrily squinted her steel blue eyes, slowly turned around, and said, "Jason, did something happen to my ice cream?"

I said, "No, your ice cream is fine."

She said, "Then why does it taste like motor oil? Son, did you drop my ice cream?"

I said nonchalantly, "Yeah, but then I picked it up and put it back on the cone so you could eat it."

"Are you serious?" she asked.

"Yes," I sincerely replied. "Why? Is there a problem?" I made a terrible mistake but not for the wrong reasons. I genuinely thought I was doing the right thing and thought I did it well.

Perhaps it was the innocent look, long curly brown hair, or the blue eyes of her six-year-old son. But something prevented my mother's wrath from erupting. Something defused the situation. She had to make an important decision between two opposing forces. Would she give in to feelings of anger? Or would she forgive me?

To this day, we laugh about what happened, although I laugh more than she does. Had her ice cream fallen into something toxic, the story could have ended differently. Imagine if the piece of glass had gotten wedged in her throat. She could have been seriously injured. Some parents would have exploded at their children for doing such a brainless thing. Instead, my mom chose to forgive me.

Previously, we learned that transformation begins

only when we have a legitimate reason for change. I call it discovering our *why*. Once we grab onto a strong enough reason to change, we form a relationship with God and look to Him to change our perspective. With that changed perspective, He helps us break destructive cycles that hold us back. Then we establish godly habits that replace the destructive ones.

This chapter deals with the fifth step in our life-changing journey. We will learn the importance of avoiding bitterness and anger and of letting go of our past hurts. Specifically, we will talk about the significance of forgiving others and the freedom we experience when we receive forgiveness. Once we complete this step, our lives will take on new power, meaning, and significance.

BITTERNESS AND ANGER CREATE INROADS FOR THE ENEMY

Something happens to us when we do not release our anger and forgive those who have hurt us. Interestingly, our anger has no effect on anyone else (unless we express it), but it does have a devastating effect on us. Like a cancerous tumor that eats away at vital organs, if left unattended, bitterness and anger consume our soul.

Scripture says, "'In your anger do not sin': Do not

let the sun go down while you are still angry, and do not give the devil a foothold" (Eph. 4:26–27). When we allow the sun to go down while we are still angry, in essence, we forfeit our freedom. How? Holding onto anger gives the devil an inroad into our lives, and as a result, we become enslaved to vicious cycles. Our anger opens the door to bitterness. Bitterness opens the door to spite. Spite opens the door to contempt.

Since 2001, at each of my crusades we have had a special area designated for counseling. Approximately 70 percent of the people who ask to talk with one of our counselors have something or someone they have never been able to forgive. Whether they have marital issues, family problems, or feelings of depression, it doesn't take the counselor long to find an area of bitterness. In virtually every case, the conflict took place between two people. Some carry the resentment and hatred not for years, but for decades. Instead of getting over the past and closing the door to the enemy, they insist on keeping it wide open.

With time, the inroads become highways. People who hold onto their bitterness and anger grow more negative and pessimistic and find it difficult to trust others. They tend to have unhealthy friendships and dysfunctional family relationships. They become more and more secluded. It pains me to see so many people who seem powerless to let go of the hurts and frustrations that keep them in bondage.

Over the years, I have noticed several devastating consequences for those who don't get past the past. These are the results of bitterness that we continue to harbor.

THE RESULTS OF BITTERNESS

1. It's Poisonous

Bitterness is like a poison we drink hoping that someone else will die, but it winds up killing us instead. Harboring bitterness always does more damage to us than to the people we hold in contempt. It gnaws away at us, slowly tears us down, and destroys us. As Scripture says, "For I see that you are full of bitterness and captive to sin" (Acts 8:23).

A missionary colleague told me a story about a woman in Africa who had a son. The son got married, and his wife didn't get along with his mother. After several years of tiptoeing around each other, his wife and his mother had a brutal fight. From that time forward, they didn't speak to each other.

Whenever the son's mother talked about her daughter-in-law, she became enraged, and bitterness consumed her heart. Every day she thought of new ways to lash out at her son's wife. It wasn't long before she started rumors, saying that her daughter-in-law was being unfaithful to her son, was abusing the grandchildren, and was spending all their money.

One day, the son's mother grew ill, to the point that she was bedridden. For weeks, the family doctor ran tests but could not find anything physically wrong with her. Slowly but surely her body was shutting down, and no one knew why. The doctor noticed one consistency in every visit, however. Whenever he asked the question, "So how's the family?" she would answer the same way, "Everyone is fine except for my son. He suffers so much being married to that wicked woman."

After several weeks, the doctor finally decided to give the family a recommendation for a different type of treatment. "In my opinion, she doesn't need a medical doctor," he said. "She needs a spiritual one, someone who can help her get over her anger." He recommended she talk with the pastor who lived nearby. With their permission, the doctor set up a time for a pastoral visit. The family agreed, and the next day, the pastor came at noon.

When the pastor walked into the room, he asked the woman, "Tell me, what's going on in your life?"

"Besides being confined to this bed, I'm doing fine," she replied.

"Tell me, how's the rest of your family?"

Almost on cue, the woman rolled her eyes and said, "Funny you should ask." Then she began ranting about her daughter-in-law.

The pastor said, "Well, I think I've found the source of your problem."

"Yes," the woman blurted out. "She is the source of all my problems, and if I could get out of this bed, I'd make her pay for it."

The pastor said, "Well, there is a way for you to get out of that bed, and it won't cost you anything for the prescription. As a matter of fact, the only way you'll ever get out of that bed is by forgiving your daughter-in-law."

"What?" the woman exclaimed. "Did you say, 'Forgive her'?"

"That's exactly what I said," the pastor replied.

"Why in the world should I forgive her?" the woman asked.

"Because that's the only way you'll experience freedom from the pain that has enslaved you," he said. "God has not made our physical bodies to endure bitterness for an extended period of time. Eventually we break down if we do not forgive those who have offended us."

Although the woman resisted at first, the pastor

convinced her to say the words *I forgive you,* followed by her daughter-in-law's name. After praying, he exhorted her not to fall back into the trap of pondering on painful emotions. She followed his wise and godly counsel, and by the end of the next day, she was back on her feet. She called her daughter-in-law and expressed her desire to meet with her. That night they talked and wept together, reconciling their differences.

Doctors tell us that in many cases, heart attacks and strokes are caused when people leave their anger and bitterness unresolved and bottled up.[1] They also tell us that many modern-day diseases are the result of stress-related issues.[2] When we refuse to forgive and release those who have hurt us, the damage it does to us is far greater than anything we could hope to inflict upon them. Besides, if we refuse to release those who have hurt us, bitterness spreads from our hearts and infects those who are close to us.

2. It's Contagious

Bitterness passes from one person to another like a sickness. In chapter 2, we talked about the things that we learn and pass on to the next generation.

Bitterness is a learned behavior as well. We pick it up from our parents, coworkers, friends, family, and other influential persons. And if we can pick it up, we can spread it around. As Scripture warns us, "See to it that no one misses the grace of God and that no bitter root grows up to cause trouble and defile many" (Heb. 12:15).

Before I became a missionary, I worked as a sales representative for a large multinational corporation. I made a good salary. They gave me a desk with a view of the beautiful water fountain that sat between the brand new office buildings. They provided a decent medical and dental plan. As a twenty-one-year-old, I was excited to be a part of the largest company in their industry. Within weeks, though, I noticed that my high level of excitement was plummeting.

It started as I rounded the corner each morning heading toward the water cooler at break time. At first, other employees lowered their voices when I approached, but soon I gained their confidence and they let me in on the topic of conversation. Why all the secrecy? Several of the employees felt the company was incompetent in some areas.

They complained that the compensation package was too low. They were dissatisfied with the company's performance. Other companies could deliver a less expensive product much quicker then we could. Soon, the employees had a laundry list of complaints, and with time it grew.

Before long, I chimed in as well. I found myself complaining about my salary, stubborn manufacturers, and the management team. The attitude of bitterness was contagious, and it had infected me. I allowed what I heard to change my perception of the company, and bitterness crept in. What's worse, my attitude was having a negative effect on newer employees.

In time, many sales representatives moved on to other organizations, and after eighteen months, one young woman and I were the senior reps in the office. She and I made a commitment to halt all negative conversations in an effort to turn around the office morale. Until they shut down our division, we managed to put the past in the past and made the office a positive place where sales reps could excel at their jobs.

Bitterness acts like a virus that spreads from person to person. Before we know it, it's touched everyone close to us. Unfortunately it doesn't wear off. Instead, it gets worse with time. Perhaps the most overlooked effect of being bitter is its longevity. It can stick with us for years.

3. It's Binding

Bitterness keeps us firmly bonded to those who have offended us until the day we make a choice to release them. People say that time heals everything. Not so!

We experience healing from bitterness only when we make a conscious choice to be free. Have you ever been at a family reunion where some of the people have been through a divorce? Ask someone about his or her ex, and you'll see just how much healing has come to his or her life as a result of time.

Recently I spoke to a man who went through a divorce over thirty years ago. He was an admitted workaholic who was less than attentive to his wife. She grew tired of feeling alone in the relationship. So she called it quits. The dispute was intense. In the settlement, she got the kids and the house. Four years later, she married again. He carried the pain of rejection for three decades. Sadly, after all those years, he never remarried.

Over a cup of coffee, he confessed to me that occasionally he asks mutual friends what his ex-wife is up to. When he hears that things are difficult, he feels a sense of twisted joy. When things are going well, he reluctantly says, "Well, good for her." But deep down inside, he is disappointed that his ex-wife is happy without him. He wishes she still had feelings for him.

Ironic, isn't it? A man can love a woman, hate a woman, and hope that calamity touches her life. He can harbor bitterness in his heart for years, even decades. And bitterness, not love, is what keeps him bound to her.

Bitterness is a dangerous emotional glue that keeps us connected in an unhealthy way to those who have hurt us. If we want to experience true freedom from the pain of the past, we need to release those who have hurt us.

What about you? Have you been hurt by others and still find it difficult to forgive them? Do you have difficulty letting go of your past? Has Satan made an inroad into your life?

I want you to know that you're not a bad person if you answered yes to these questions. At any given moment in life, we encounter people who mistreat us, and it's normal to feel hurt. The good news is we don't have to continue suffering. We can experience freedom. We can experience true power, and the Lord will show us how.

THE SOLUTION

Whether you want to be a better Christian, advance in your career, lose weight, or become financially secure, God says change is possible. These things are attainable. With God, all things are possible, but only if you follow His prescription for change. God offers you power to change the things you want to be different, but it's tied directly to your ability to forgive those who have offended you. What does forgiveness have to do with advancing and excelling in different areas of your life? Forgiveness breaks us free from the weights that keep us from moving forward. And nothing weighs us down like the chains of bitterness and anger. That is why Scripture encourages us to "get rid of all bitterness, rage and anger, brawling and slander, along with every form of malice" (Eph. 4:31).

Jesus understood the power of forgiveness. To Him, forgiving others was vital for a life filled with freedom and significance. Forgiveness was so important that He made it contingent on our willingness to forgive others. He shared this expectation with the disciples on two different occasions. The first is found in the Gospel of Matthew: "For if you forgive men when they sin against you, your heavenly Father will also forgive you. But if you do not forgive men their sins, your Father will not forgive your sins" (Matt. 6:14–15).

Second, Christ gave us an example of how our attitude of forgiveness should be directly tied to the way we pray. In Luke 11:2–4, He explains to His disciples, "When you pray, say: "'Father, hallowed be your name, your kingdom come. Give us each day our daily bread. Forgive us our sins, for we also forgive everyone who sins against us. And lead us not into temptation.'"

In this prayer, extending forgiveness to others opens the door for us to ask God to forgive us. We have the privilege of asking God to forgive us because we are in the process of forgiving those who have offended us. The opposite is true if we refuse to forgive. It closes the door to God's forgiveness and opens the door to the enemy of our soul.

When Peter heard Jesus' teaching on forgiveness, he asked, "'Lord, how many times shall I forgive my brother when he sins against me? Up to seven times?' Jesus answered, 'I tell you, not seven times, but seventy-seven times'" (Matt. 18:21–22). I find Peter's question humorous. Down deep inside, I would be asking the same thing. The Lord's response must have seemed overwhelming. Jesus wasn't referring to sheer numbers, though. He was saying that forgiveness is an attitude, a lifestyle, a daily choice.

Then in Matthew 18, Jesus told His disciples a story about a rich master. Times were difficult, and the wealthy man wanted to reconcile his finances. One after another, he called each of his servants to give an account of the money they owed him. One in particular owed millions of dollars. When the master asked him how he was going to pay off the debt, the servant replied, "I do not have the means to repay you."

The master became enraged and ordered that the

servant's entire family be sold as slaves to pay off the debt. The servant was heartbroken and fell to his knees. He begged his master to spare his family the grief and humiliation. He said, "Be patient with me... and I will pay back everything" (v. 26).

Seeing that the servant was greatly distressed, the master felt sorry for him. He said, "I forgive your debts. You are a free man."

Later, the servant was walking down the street with a spring in his step when suddenly he bumped into a fellow servant. The fellow servant owed him only a hundred dollars. The first servant said, "Hey, where is that money you owe me?" Then he grabbed his fellow servant by the neck and started to choke him. "You will pay me back everything you owe!" Then he did the unthinkable. After refusing to listen to the fellow servant's plea for an extension, he ordered that he be thrown into prison until he could pay his debt.

The other servants who were watching felt that the first servant had acted harshly and unjustly. So they went to their master and told him everything that happened. The master was angry, and called the servant to give an account of his actions. He said, "You wicked servant. I cancelled all your debt. Why didn't you forgive your fellow servant in the same way I forgave you?" The master then gave the order to have the servant thrown into jail to be tortured until he could repay everything that he owed.

Then Jesus emphatically said to His disciples, "This is how my heavenly Father will treat each of you unless you forgive your brother from your heart" (v. 35).

Why does the Lord place such a high importance on our willingness to forgive those who have offended us? He wants us to experience true freedom. Forgiving others isn't necessarily for their benefit, it's for ours. It isn't for their health, it's for ours. It's not for their freedom, it's for ours. Besides, He didn't ask us to do something that He wasn't prepared to do as well. We are told, "Bear with each other and forgive whatever grievances you may have against one another. Forgive as the Lord forgave you" (Col. 3:13).

God expresses His love to us by forgiving our sins. In essence, He said, "I will forgive humans for all that they have done: adultery, fornication, impurity and debauchery; idolatry and witchcraft; hatred, discord, jealousy, fits of rage, selfish ambition, dissensions, factions and envy; drunkenness and orgies." The only condition for receiving forgiveness, aside from asking God for it, is to forgive others as He has forgiven us.

It's important to mention that if you feel you are in a dangerous situation either emotionally or physically, you need to contact someone who can help you move out of harm's way. You can forgive someone without being at risk. Just because we forgive someone doesn't mean that we continue to allow others to inflict pain upon us. We must take the proper steps to ensure our safety.

Thus far, we've discovered the consequences for harboring bitterness and anger toward those who have offended us. We've studied Christ's remedy and model for forgiveness. Talking about forgiveness and taking action are two different things, however. So how do we forgive when it can be so challenging? How do we experience true freedom from the past?

CRUCIAL STEPS TO FORGIVENESS

This brings us to the most important question of this chapter. How do we forgive people who have hurt us? There are several practical things we need to keep in mind. First of all, we must recognize that forgiveness is not an emotion. *It's a decision.* We make the choice to release those who have hurt us. Feelings can be misleading, especially when it comes to pain. So we need to make sure that our choices are guided by our ability to think clearly. In every case, forgiveness boils down to a choice, and once we decide, we don't reverse our decision.

Over the years, I've talked with couples who have dealt with marital infidelity. In the cases where one spouse has been unfaithful, the marriage can experience a healthy recovery depending upon the other spouse's ability to forgive. If he or she was able to forgive the spouse and let go of the past whenever reminded of the error, their relationship healed and deepened. Spouses who cannot forgive one another eventually find themselves barely surviving, because the lack of forgiveness produces a high level of mistrust and paranoia.

Second, forgiveness is not an option. *It's a command.* Wherever the concept of forgiveness is mentioned in Scripture, it is never associated with a feeling or a suggestion. It's used as a verb and given in the form of a mandate. "Be even-tempered, content with second place, quick to forgive an offense. Forgive as quickly and completely as the Master forgave you" (Col. 3:13 *The Message*). "Be alert. If you see your friend going wrong, correct him. If he responds, forgive him. Even if it's personal against you and repeated seven times through the day, and seven times he says, 'I'm sorry, I won't do it again,' forgive him" (Luke 17:3–4 *The Message*).

Third, forgiveness is not usually instantaneous. *It's an ongoing process.* There will be days when we remember what someone did to us and recall the pain he or she caused. For that reason, days, months, even years after the incident, we still have feelings of betrayal. During those times, we must remind ourselves that we are in a process of putting the past in the past. Although we can't deny the way we feel, we can tell ourselves that each day we choose to live a healthy, bitterness-free life.

Fourth, we remember that when we feel over-whelmed by the betrayal of others, *the Lord will help us through the difficulty*. He is there to lighten our load. Jesus said, "Take my yoke upon you and learn from me, for I am gentle and humble in heart, and you will find rest for your souls" (Matt. 11:29). The Lord invites us to cast aside the heavy burdens we carry in exchange for His light load. If you want to live a fruitful life and experience all that God wants for you, then practice forgiveness. Release your anger, bitter-ness, and hurt to the Lord. Give it all to God, and let Him carry your burdens.

The fifth and final aspect of forgiveness is an action that will greatly help in your quest for true freedom. *Your decision to forgive is something you can write out or say out loud.* If you have come to the point where you want to be set free from all bitterness and anger, if you want to break free from the chains that have kept you bound to those who have caused you pain and anguish, if today is the day you want to experience freedom from a stifled life of being stuck in your cyclone of anger, take a piece of paper and write out a prayer to the Lord asking for His help to forgive your offenders. Then toward the end, list their names and in an audible voice, say, "[Insert first name], I forgive you." Do this for each person who has caused you pain.

Once you make a commitment through prayer to forgive, with time your emotions will reflect the choice you have made. You will feel less angry and bitter toward those who have hurt you. If you find it difficult to say the words of forgiveness, then stop, back up, and ask God to help you. He will. Ask Him to take away your burden and replace it with His. You will find that after a short time, the heaviness you carry will lighten and what seemed to be an impossible feat will be manageable.

Recently, I had a conversation with Richard Larson, a man who pastored a church in Panama from 1970 to 1978. He had a television program that was on three nights a week. On one particular program, Larson shared a story from a book entitled *None of These Diseases* in which the author wrote about a couple who moved out of the city to retire in a small town to lead a quiet life.[3]

After a few months, however, the couple became bored and decided to start raising chickens as a hobby.

Soon the chickens started laying eggs, and before they knew it, they had an egg business. The small business kept them occupied and developed into something meaningful they could do with their spare time.

Everything was fine until a young man who graduated from the university with a degree in agriculture returned to his hometown to start a commercial egg business. He acquired new and sophisticated equipment and bought enough chickens to start producing eggs. Soon his business out-produced all the other farmers in town. Eventually, people stopped buying eggs from the older couple and started buying from the young entrepreneur.

The older couple became frustrated. In their minds, this was a violation of common courtesy. The young businessman never took into account what was happening to their business. Although they were retired and producing eggs as a hobby, they felt the young man had invaded their turf. The thing they enjoyed during their retirement was taken from them.

Within a short time, they started having health problems. The husband went to the doctor, but nothing conclusive was found. The doctor started asking questions about their lifestyle and discovered that the man was bitter over the young entrepreneur who took away all their business.

The doctor said, "Well, you have to choose between your health and holding a grudge. My recommendation is that you let it go. If you don't, this is going to wind up killing you. Who knows, perhaps the three of you might consider working together, if you still want something to do."

The older man didn't like what the doctor said, but he decided to go home and talk it over with his wife. After thinking about it, he came to the conclusion, "Since I'm an accountant, maybe we could be helpful and give the young man some business advice."

The elderly couple approached the young man and offered him assistance, and he kindly accepted their offer. Their health problems began to disappear.

As Larson finished the story, he looked into the camera and said, "There is someone watching me tonight who is in big trouble, and it's because you are not forgiving someone who has hurt you. Maybe that person has done something that you would say is unforgiveable. Maybe it's really bad, but if you don't forgive that person it's going to destroy you, maybe even kill you." Then he prayed and closed the program. The show aired a week later on a Monday night.

The following Thursday, Larson's assistant received a phone call. The voice on the other end of the phone said, "Please send the pastor to the hospital. I need to speak to him at once!" The assistant conveyed the message to the pastor who rushed to the Panamanian hospital. After walking down the corridor, he found the room and walked in.

There, sitting on the edge of the hospital bed, was a man with a smile on his face. At first, Larson wondered if he was in the right room. *If this man is dying, why is he smiling? And why did I rush down here for nothing?* he thought.

Then the man said, "Let me tell you what happened. A while back, I went to Europe on a business trip. I was gone for a month. When I came back, I discovered that my wife ran away with my best friend. I then had one thing on my mind—destroying their lives. I became so angry and so bitter, and I soon became deathly ill.

"The doctors diagnosed me with a rare form of leukemia. There were only a few known cases of the type I had. They told me that the only hope for decent treatment would be in New York or in Europe, but I couldn't afford that. So I wound up checking into this hospital."

The man went on to explain that as he was lying in bed watching television, he heard Larson tell the story about the chicken farmer. He heard the exhortation toward the end of the program. Then he knelt by the side of his bed and asked God to help him forgive his wife and best friend. As soon as he finished praying, he felt as if a huge load had been lifted off his shoulders. He felt clean inside. He felt like a new person.

The next morning, the doctors took some blood for testing, and they returned later in the day with the results. They were shocked to report that the leukemia was gone. They said, "We don't know what happened. We don't understand this form of leukemia well, but it seems to have disappeared." Then they took more tests, but they all came back the same.

Larson later told me that the doctors were not certain what happened to that man prior to his visit to the hospital. One thing is certain, though. After he asked God for the power to forgive, his body began to function normally.

As I mentioned earlier, forgiveness is a decision, not an emotion. It is a daily choice. It's realizing that if Jesus could forgive us for all that we have done to Him, then surely we can forgive others. As the Bible says, "Be kind and compassionate to one another, forgiving each other, just as in Christ God forgave you" (Eph. 4:32).

THE BEAST IN THE BEAUTY

The crowd started to head for the exits after we concluded the last night of an overseas crusade. My ministerial coordinator approached me by the side of the stage and told me that a few of the ushers wanted me to pray for them individually. I was more than happy to do so, since they had faithfully served thousands of people during the weeklong event. As our team disassembled the sound and lighting systems, I asked each usher how I could pray for his or her specific needs.

I came to a young woman who had her eyes closed. As I approached her to find out how I might pray for her, she let out a bloodcurdling scream.

Everyone froze. We all focused on her, wondering what would happen next. Nothing was said for three seconds, but her face reflected a diabolical anger.

With her eyes still closed, she took a swipe at me with her nails. Then she took a deep breath and screamed.

She dropped to the ground and backpedaled away from me, throwing sand in the air. Then she covered her ears and screamed, "No! No!" Fortunately, we had people there who were trained to help with the situation. Several individuals picked her up and carried her to a separate location, where our counseling and prayer team could attend to her needs.

About twenty minutes later, she came to her senses. That's when she confessed several disturbing things about her life. She had been forced into prostitution when she was younger. She lived a life of drugs and abuse in a marginalized community and learned to hate men.

Two weeks before the crusade, she walked into a local church where the pastor announced that our ministry needed volunteers for the event. So she raised her hand and offered to help. Prior to that, she had no relationship with Christ and apparently never had forgiven those who had abused her. The wounds and emotional damage opened the door of her heart to hatred and bitterness. Satan found an inroad.

The counselor sat down with her and explained the importance of forgiveness. She told her, "Forgiveness is not an emotion. It's a decision. You must decide to forgive every day."

During the time of prayer that followed, the young lady audibly spoke the names of the men who had hurt, raped, and abused her. Then she came to the most difficult bridge of all. She verbalized her forgiveness toward the one man who had caused so much pain when she was younger, the one who forced her into prostitution.

Once she made the breakthrough, her life changed dramatically. During the days that followed, she began to experience a newfound freedom. She started attending her local church and since that time has had no reoccurrences of what she experienced that night.

Indeed, Jesus has come to set the captive free. He comes to give us life and take away the torment that keeps us in survival mode. He says in John 10:10: "The thief comes only to steal and kill and destroy; I have come that they may have life, and have it to the full." This is God's desire and plan for us. He wants us to live life, not just survive it. The only way we can live life to its fullest is by cutting the ties that keep us bound by bitterness and anger. The only way to be free from bitterness and anger is to forgive. As painful and as unjust as it may sound, forgiveness is the only way to true freedom. Only when we forgive those who have hurt us can we experience life without chains.

Is there someone in your life you need to forgive? When you remember the incident—the lies, the betrayal, the unfaithfulness—do you become angry the way you did the first time? If so, don't wait to take action. Take the power that God offers you and use it to experience true freedom.

The principles of forgiveness are universally applicable. Whether we need to forgive others, deal with the pent-up anger we have toward God, or move beyond our self-hatred, releasing our bitterness is necessary in order to get past the past.

Thus far, we've talked about forgiving others, a process that is a cornerstone for change. The last part of this chapter deals with the importance of asking others for forgiveness.

WIPING THE SLATE CLEAN

The Bible tells us, "Be kind and compassionate to one another, forgiving each other, just as in Christ God forgave you" (Eph. 4:32). It's one thing to extend forgiveness to those who have offended us. It's another thing entirely to push our pride to one side and ask someone to forgive us. For some reason, the most difficult sentence to say is "I was wrong, forgive me." Something incredible happens, though, when we ask to be pardoned. It rebuilds broken relationships and opens the door to our restoration with God.

God anointed David king over Israel and delivered him from the hand of Saul. God gave him everything a king could want or need. The Lord told him that He would have given him even more. So what possessed David to send a man to his death just so that he could cover up an adulterous affair?

When he stood on top of his roof gazing out over his kingdom on that sleepless spring night, David couldn't help but notice the young woman bathing on her patio. Her name was Bathsheba, a woman of great beauty. The voyeur wasn't the only one enjoying the show. Surely she knew David was watching her. When he summoned Bathsheba to spend time with him at the palace, she agreed to go without hesitation.

After their brief sexual encounter, David sent her home. Weeks passed, and she sent word to him saying that she was pregnant. Immediately, he devised a scheme to cover up his sin. He sent a message to the military commander in the field where her husband was stationed: "Send me Uriah the Hittite!"

David's plan was to persuade Uriah to go home to be with his wife, so that Uriah would think that the baby was his child. But Uriah was a soldier who had strong convictions. Instead of spending time with his wife, he chose to sleep at the palace entrance with the rest of the servants of the king. The next day, David invited him to dinner and made him stay until he was drunk. Then he sent him home. Still, Uriah slept at the entrance of the palace with the other servants.

David's plan failed. Uriah never slept with his wife, and Bathsheba's sinful encounter with David was one step closer to blowing up in their faces. Out of desperation, the king did something horrific. He ordered his commander, Joab, to put Uriah on the front lines and abandon him during battle. Joab followed the orders, and Uriah was killed trying to faithfully defend the king who had slept with his wife and maliciously sent him to his death.

Up until Uriah's death, David could have set the record straight. He could have wiped the slate clean, but he didn't. Instead, he tried to hide his sin. He refused to repent, and this angered the Lord.

In response to his wicked behavior, God sent a prophet named Nathan to confront the king and his twisted heart. Nathan told David everything that he had done. Then he told him what God was going to do because of his lack of repentance.

God said,

> "Now, therefore, the sword will never depart from your house, because you despised me and took the wife of Uriah the Hittite to be your own." This is what the LORD says: "Out of your own household I am going to bring calamity upon you. Before your very eyes I will take your wives and give them to one who is close to you, and he will lie with your wives in broad daylight. You did it in secret, but I will do

this thing in broad daylight before all Israel."
(2 Samuel 12:10–12)

When David heard the Lord's verdict, he quickly changed his attitude. He broke down and said, "I have sinned against the LORD" (v. 13). By repenting, David spared his own life, but he couldn't save the life of the son born to Bathsheba. After the boy was born, he was stricken with an illness and within seven days he died.

David was a believer. He had a relationship with God. He worshiped Him and studied His laws. Yet in spite of his outstanding connection to the Lord, he failed miserably and tried to cover it up. His selfish actions caused a chain reaction that took the lives of two other innocent people. When David realized there was nowhere to hide, he quickly admitted his sin. He wiped the slate clean, and his repentance brought about his redemption once again.

The consequences of our stubbornness can be fatal. The repercussions for our refusal to ask for forgiveness can be detrimental to our well-being and to those around us. If we turn our hearts to the Lord and wipe the slate clean, he is faithful to forgive all our transgressions.

Are there things that you're trying to cover up?

Do you need to set the record straight with someone or with God? Do you have trouble sleeping at night because you haven't come clean about a mistake you've made or a sin you've committed? When you hide your mistakes, you simply prolong the inevitable. If you feel there are issues you need to clear up, you don't have to spend your days and nights looking over your shoulder. There is a better way. God's way can help you experience the peace you seek. So what do you need to do? Come clean.

SETTING THE RECORD STRAIGHT

God wants us to set the record straight with those we have offended. He does not want us to run from our responsibility. This requires that we swallow our pride. We may feel the urge to be defensive and start pointing a finger. That only makes things worse and keeps us from walking in the blessings of God. Instead, remember that the quickest way to freedom is to come clean and tell the truth.

⚭

Several years ago, Valerie, an attractive high school student, found Christ and started attending a church a few miles from her house. Her parents were not religious, but they supported her new life. Within two years, Valerie became a leader in the youth group. She had a special gift for reaching out to the students in her high school. Because of her evangelistic heart, many young people found Christ.

One day, she met a handsome young doctor. Their flirtatious conversation led to a first date, where he told her that he was single. With his blond hair and blue eyes, the young man quickly swept her off her feet. The two began seeing each other occasionally.

That year, he rented a villa in the mountains and asked her to join him for a romantic getaway. She enthusiastically agreed and told her parents that she was heading to a weekend retreat with her church.

Six weeks later, she discovered that her rendez-vous had life-changing consequences. She was pregnant. Valerie sadly realized there was no easy way out. Questions flooded her mind. *What will my parents think? What will my church think? What will all the young people think?*

To make matters worse, when she told her boy-friend, he told her the truth: he had a wife and children. What seemed to be a romance made in heaven turned out to be a nightmare concocted in hell.

In the weeks that followed, Valerie tried to rationalize her mistake by focusing on what she felt were inconsistencies in the church. Instead of coming clean, she pointed her finger at the leadership and spread rumors about all the hypocrites.

After a few months, she could no longer hide her error. She told her parents what happened, and soon the church found out as well. Because of her leadership position in youth ministry, the pastor and board called her into a meeting. She anticipated the battle of her life.

The night of the meeting, Valerie sat alone just outside the conference room. She felt that the leaders were plotting against her. She expected that they were prejudging her and planning everything they were going to say. She went over in her mind how she would respond and would put them in their place.

Finally the boardroom door opened and someone said, "Valerie, the board is ready to see you now." She clenched her jaw and stood to her feet. As she walked through the door, the members were standing to receive her. They respectfully greeted her and then returned to their seats.

The pastor folded his hands in front of him on the conference table and said, "Well, there is no easy way to say this. We know that God loves us in spite of our mistakes, and He forgives us no matter what we do. What you've done is no secret. Valerie, we are disappointed in your behavior. This is not becoming of you. What's worse, you've lied to everyone and have deceived the members of your own youth group. Do you have anything to say for yourself?"

Valerie was nervous, but she was ready for a fight. She took a deep breath and said with a slight quiver in her voice, "Yes, I have something to say. I am not the only one who makes mistakes. This church is full of hypocrites. This board is no exception. Everything that is said in these board meetings is leaked to the rest of the congregation. Nothing is sacred anymore! What do *you* have to say for yourselves?"

The members quietly listened to her rambling. When she finished her tirade, silence filled the room.

Then the woman sitting next to her leaned over, put her arm around her, and softly said, "If you only knew how much we love you and how much we have prayed for you, you wouldn't say any of those things."

Valerie was stunned. Tears came to her eyes and then streamed down her cheeks. Within seconds, she covered her face and cried, "I am so sorry for what I have done. I don't know what I was thinking." The members of the board quickly gathered around and embraced her. Someone distributed tissues to dry the many tears that were shed.

Valerie then looked into the pastor's eyes and said,

"I would like to go before the congregation and ask for their forgiveness as well. I need to set the record straight with everyone, especially the young people in this church."

The pastor agreed, and on the following Sunday, Valerie stood on the platform and told the church what had happened. She asked for their forgiveness for her illicit affair and for spreading gossip. When she finished, the church surrounded her with an outpouring of love. Seven months later, the women of that church threw Valerie one of the biggest baby showers ever.

Valerie was reconciled not only because of the church's willingness to forgive her, but for her willingness to ask them for forgiveness. She was transformed by following God's leading in asking for forgiveness. Valerie tapped into the real power of God by coming clean and making things right with those she had offended.

You may be saying, "It's too late for me. I've made too many mistakes. The damage is done. Innocent people will be hurt if I reveal what I've done." It's true. There are times when the debts we've incurred cannot be covered by us alone. That's when we need someone to help us resolve our conflicts. We need God's help to get out of our mess.

Listen, friend, there is no difficulty too great that

God can't help you through. There is nothing too catastrophic that God can't help you resolve. No matter what you've done, God can help you put your life back together again. When you're in over your head, ask God for help.

BRING ME THE CHECK

When I worked as a sales representative, my territory covered a large area of Orange County, California. One day, to avoid the traffic, I arrived in the vicinity of my customer's office about an hour early. I pulled off the freeway and found a spot in a parking structure in a mall close to my sales call. My appointment was at 11:00 a.m.

While I waited, I leaned the car seat back and turned on some soft music. Before long, I fell asleep. Several hours passed, and about 2:00 p.m., I finally woke up. I was completely disoriented and stumbled out of the car and headed across the parking lot to a restaurant. My missed appointment never crossed my mind.

The friendly hostess greeted me at the door, settled me in a booth by the window, and handed me a menu.

When the server came to take my order, I said,

"Tell me, what plate has the most amount of food on it?" She said, "Well that would be the Tostada Salad." I asked, "What's in it?" She said, "It has everything."

I was famished, so I said, "I'll take it." She politely took the menu and headed for the kitchen. I eagerly awaited my feast.

A few minutes passed and she emerged from the kitchen bringing the most beautiful culinary creation I had seen in some time. It looked like a mountain of sizzling beef, pork, and chicken lying atop a bed of lettuce and refried beans. At the base of the volcano, there was a thick layer of sour cream. Everything was resting in a huge tortilla shell. To top it off, they had sprinkled cheddar and mozzarella cheese that covered the meat like snow blanketing the Rockies in February.

I thanked the Lord for the food and dug in like the Tasmanian Devil. About five minutes into my culinary adventure, I remembered I had no money. I was broke. I had no credit cards, no cash, and in those days, no one had cellular phones. I woke up at that moment.

When I was a teenager, I worked as a dishwasher in a restaurant. One time a couple came in and couldn't pay their bill. The manager placed them under citizen's arrest. As I sat there without any money, I thought, *The manager is going to arrest me.* Although I was distraught over how I was going to pay the bill, I continued to eat.

It's interesting, isn't it? Many times we find ourselves doing what we know is going to push us further into trouble. By the time I had finished most of the food, I had painted my way into a corner, and there was no way out. That's when I prayed. "I really need Your help, Lord. I have no money. I have no credit cards. I have no way to get hold of someone who can help. Help me, please."

At that moment, I looked down and spotted something. There, lying on top of a piece of lettuce was a tiny, curly black hair.

At that moment, the server returned and said, "How is everything?" "Everything is great. Except for the fact that there is a tiny hair right here," I said as I pointed to it. She looked at the plate and almost gagged. She said, "Oh my goodness! That's terrible! I will take care of this right away!"

She grabbed the plate and rushed through the kitchen doors. Since the restaurant was fairly empty, I could hear her raise her voice and slam the plate down on the counter.

A few minutes later, she returned and said, "I am so sorry. We really want to make this up to you. What would you like in place of the Tostada Salad?"

At that point I had eaten most of my meal, and I really wasn't hungry. So I said, "The truth of the matter is, I no longer have an appetite."

She said, "Well, sir, the restaurant has decided to cover the cost of your meal."

I said, "No! No! That is not necessary. I insist on paying." (As if I had any way to do so!) She said, "I am sorry, sir, but the manager has already written off your meal. If you were to pay for it now, it would throw off our accounting system."

My bill had been paid. My debt had been forgiven. The restaurant had cleared me of all charges, and I walked out of there a free man.

In the same way, Christ paid a bill that you and I are incapable of paying. The Bible says, "You were bought at a price; do not become slaves of men" (1 Cor. 7:23). Because He forgives our sins, we can walk freely without the spiritual burdens that weigh us down. Only Jesus can clear us of the charges.

Perhaps you have never asked the Lord for forgiveness for things that you have done. Maybe you have done things that no one knows about, and you carry deep-rooted guilt. There is a way to experience true freedom from the past, and now is the perfect time to experience it. You don't have to continue carrying the load. The burdens from the past do not have to be a permanent part of who you are. You can be free from all that holds you back, especially your past mistakes.

God is your friend, and extends His helping hand to you right now. He offers you forgiveness. So take it, and allow Him to work in you. Through this process, you will see that His healing, His power, and His love are real.

Forgiving others is liberating and empowering. Failure to forgive keeps us emotionally connected to those who hurt us. And asking for forgiveness is crucial to the spirit and soul. Experiencing forgiveness is transforming. It releases a great burden that we carry.

⚬✷⚬

As we close this chapter, ask the Lord to give you the strength to forgive the people you need to forgive. If there is anything hidden in your heart that you need to confess to the Lord, take a few moments and ask Him to help you clean the slate by praying this prayer:

Lord, I know that I have not lived a perfect life. I'm sure there have been times when I have hurt You, and I ask You to forgive me. I also ask You to forgive me for hurting other people— those in past relationships, those in my family, and people who were once my friends. As I ask

You to clear all the charges against me, I consciously decide to forgive everyone who has hurt me. Just as You have forgiven me, I choose to forgive others for what they have done. Lord, give me the strength to be a forgiving person, and help me to live a life free of bitterness and anger. I ask You to give me Your burden that is light so that I can live life to the fullest. I ask these things in Your precious name. Amen.

CHAPTER 6

Overcome with the Help of Others

———— ⌒✿⌒ ————

S EVERAL YEARS AGO, my family was celebrating one
of our favorite times of the year, Christmas Eve.
Our girls—ages eight, ten, and twelve—were excited
to dress up for the holiday. Each one spent time fixing
her hair, applying lip gloss, and spraying on sparkly
glitter.

My wife, Cindee, cooked a twelve-pound turkey,
cut it into slices, and served it on the coffee table next
to the tree. She lit eight candles in the living room
and placed two of them in wall sconces. To further
enhance the holiday atmosphere, our locally grown
Christmas tree was beautifully decorated with over
eight hundred twinkling lights. It was an ideal setting
for a meaningful family night.

Once we finished dinner, we opened the Bible and read the story of Jesus' birth in Luke 2. As our Christmas Eve festivities wound down, my wife asked me to blow out the candles, which I did, and then we watched the movie *Home Alone*. At about 11:00 p.m., we retired for the evening.

The girls could hardly sleep. They knew that within a few hours, the family would begin opening presents on Christmas Day. After all, that was our family tradition.

At 7:00 a.m. the next morning, I went for a two-mile jog while the rest of the family was still asleep. As soon as I returned, my girls greeted me at the door. I would have preferred to shower before opening presents, but our girls couldn't wait two more minutes, let alone twenty. They had earned the right to proceed immediately. My youngest grabbed my hand and said, "Come on, Dad," and led me into the living room.

After an extended time of opening presents and separating the trash from the gifts, I said, "Well, I can't stand myself any longer. I've got to get in the shower." So I excused myself and headed to the master bath.

Afterwards, I stepped out of the shower, grabbed a towel, and started to dry off. I was almost finished when I heard my oldest daughter, Celina, in the living room. I could tell by her tone that something wasn't right. She yelled, "Mom, Dad, come quick!" She immediately said it again, this time adding, "There's a fire in the living room!"

When she said, "Fire in the living room," I thought, *The tree is in flames.*

Without thinking twice, I wrapped the towel around my waist and headed down the hallway. A huge mushroom of smoke billowed from the living room into the hallway. Like a half-covered superhero, I jumped from the hallway down into the living room. When I landed, I looked in the direction of the tree expecting to see an inferno. But it was intact.

Puzzled, I scanned the living room for the origin of the smoke. I glanced to my right and saw that a garland that was wrapped around the base of the wall sconce was on fire.

The flame was about twenty inches in height and was burning toward the curtains. To make matters worse, several feet above the curtains was an old wood ceiling, six inches under the hot tin roof. I knew that I had about a minute to extinguish the flame before it reached the curtains, then the ceiling. At that point, the house would be engulfed in flames.

I looked for something that I could use to put out the flame—a pillow or a sofa cushion—but nothing was nearby. Then I remembered I was wearing a wet

towel. So I ripped it off my waist, completely expos-
ing myself to the elements, and started beating the
flame in front of an audience of four ladies. After
three or four swipes, the fire was extinguished, and I
reared back and spiked the towel like a football after
a touchdown.

Nothing but smoke rose from the sconce.

There I stood, in all of my glory.

For some strange reason, time didn't pass quickly.
I turned around, and my three daughters had their
faces covered. I thought to myself, *Well, they're going
to need therapy after witnessing that*. I took a deep
breath and said, "Girls, keep your eyes covered, the
naked fireman has to get dressed." I remember walking back to my bedroom in slow motion. After that
sort of performance and saving the day, you feel pretty
good about yourself.

I got dressed and walked back to the living room.
The rancid smell of burnt garland permeated the
room. As I watched the smoke slowly clear, it dawned
upon me that someone must have been playing with
matches and started the fire. I was determined to find
the culprit. Raising my voice to make sure that everyone heard me, I said, "Someone was playing with
matches, and I want to know who it was. The only fire
that we had in this living room was the one that your

mom lit last night. Then she asked me to blow out the candles, which I did..."

At that moment, a disturbing thought crossed my mind. *Uh-oh. Oh my!*

When I went to bed the night before, I thought all the candles were out, but apparently they weren't. I approached the ones that looked illuminated, but when I looked at that particular candle from five feet away, it didn't give off any light. Its blue flame was undetectable. So I never extinguished it. The candle, hanging at eye level, burned the entire evening through Christmas morning. When it split in two, the wax spilled over the garland, and the little flame caught the Christmas decoration on fire.

Had it not been for my daughter walking by the living room that morning, the entire house might have burned to the ground. My daughter saw things I never saw, and she warned me of an impending doom.

In many ways, she performed the task of someone in an accountability group. She called my attention to something that could have brought destruction to my life. Without people to help us see the things we cannot see, something catastrophic might be right around the corner. For that reason, we need to establish a trusted group of friends to guide us when we cannot see clearly.

At the beginning of our journey, we discovered that transformation only comes when our reason for change—our *why*—is bigger than any excuse we conjure up. We quickly realized that without God's help to transform our perceptions, changing the destructive patterns in our lives is an impossible task. That's why we turned the reins of our life over to Him. After focusing on the patterns that brought us harm, we formed new and godly habits to replace the destructive ones. Then with the power we've gained through a real relationship with Christ and habits that bring blessing, we took the crucial step of letting go of the past and asking others for forgiveness.

KEEP GOOD COMPANY

Next we deal with the importance of surrounding ourselves with people who pull us up instead of tear us down. This is the sixth and final step in our transformational process. Specifically we will look at several dangers of trying to move forward without the help of godly people. We will also discuss how others' honesty and strength can empower us to break the barriers we face. Finally, we will look at characteristics of a group of trusted friends who can support us. The process you will discover in the following pages will energize your campaign for personal growth and help you soar high above the things that hold you back.

Over the years, I have noticed that there are three severe consequences of not having a trusted group of friends. Let's focus on the first consequence so that we can avoid moving in the wrong direction.

1. Without Godly Friends, We Tend to Wander Off Course

Over twenty-five years ago, a 747 left JFK International Airport and headed 4,200 miles away. After refueling in Anchorage, Alaska, it departed for another country. Shortly after takeoff, the aircraft deviated off course to the north by one degree. Over time, it drifted out of international airspace. Fighter planes scrambled to intercept the jumbo jet, because the country's defense department mistook the aircraft for a spy plane. Eventually, the aircraft flew out of that country's airspace and back over international waters.

Cruising at an altitude of thirty-five thousand feet, the crew of twenty-three along with hundreds of passengers had no idea what was about to happen. About four hours after takeoff, the airplane had wandered nearly 185 miles off course. It once again entered unapproved airspace and fighters scrambled to intercept the airliner. This time the command center ordered the destruction of the target. A missile struck the 747's fuselage, and cabin pressure was lost. The plane spiraled downward, and within minutes, it crashed into the sea. All 269 people on board, including passengers and crewmembers, were lost.[1]

Let's contemplate the consequences of making a navigational error of one degree. A one-degree error at the beginning of a flight is minuscule. After four hours of flight time (more than two thousand miles traveled), the difference was no longer minuscule—it was enormous. One hundred eighty-five miles is nearly the width of the state of California. The consequence of wandering off course was a loss of the aircraft and all those aboard. The communication failure between the control tower and flight crew resulted in one of the greatest tragedies in aviation history.

When we try to make it through life on our own without the help of others, we can also wind up in a dangerous place. Without godly correction, over time we can wander miles off course. I have watched godly men who thought they could resist temptation become entangled in the clutches of pornography. I have seen close friends who were convinced they had left a deadly vice fall back into drug addiction. I have seen too many people fall away from a wonderful relationship with the Lord. What did all of them have in common? They had no group of people to hold them accountable for their actions.

We were not created to be alone (Gen. 2:18). God intentionally made us to be a part of one body (1 Cor. 12:12). Especially when we can't see our way ahead, we need to depend on a special group of godly people who guide us over the mountains and through the valleys. Scripture tells us, "My brothers, if one of you should wander from the truth and someone should bring him back, remember this: Whoever turns a sinner from the error of his way will save him from death and cover over a multitude of sins" (James 5:19–20).

When we have no idea how to negotiate our way through the difficulties of life, a trusted group of friends is one of God's greatest gifts to us. And these friends can be helpful even when things are going well.

⁓∞⁓

Rick walked onto the open-air crusade completely stoned. At first, he hurled insults at me while I was preaching, but soon he calmed down and listened to the message. Something powerful happened in his life that night. With each step he took toward the altar, the chains that gripped his heart began to melt away. By the time he came to the front for prayer, tears were running down his cheeks.

As I prayed, he removed his ball cap and repeated the prayer of repentance. When I said "amen," he lifted his eyes toward heaven and I saw a drastic difference in his countenance. The young carpenter had experienced a powerful encounter with God. When he left the crusade, he was a different person.

The next week, he walked into a Sunday school class at a local church. He sat down, opened his Bible, and took copious notes. When the pastor asked if anyone had a question, Rick raised his hand and asked what Bible verses talked about building strength to overcome temptation. Within months, the rest of his family was attending the church as well. The news of his conversion spread throughout the entire neighborhood.

One day, he approached the church's pastor and said, "I feel God is calling me to help out in some sort of ministry. What can I do?" Although the pastor was pleased, he was somewhat reluctant. After all, Rick had never wanted to join any of the small groups in his church.

The next day, I called that pastor and said, "I have a need for someone who can coordinate the logistics for setting up our crusade equipment. I would need that person for a period of three days every two months. Do you have a volunteer?"

The pastor immediately thought of Rick, the carpenter. "I highly recommend this man," he said. "He is good with his hands. Be careful, though. Make sure that he connects well with the rest of your team. He can be somewhat of a Lone Ranger." I filed his comments away in the back of my mind and invited Rick to join the team for our outreaches.

Rick began traveling with us throughout the country, setting up and tearing down our fifty tons of crusade gear. The last night of each crusade, he stood on the stage in front of thousands of people and gave his testimony. He passionately shared how God delivered him from a life of drugs and gang violence. Crowds were deeply moved by the genuine story of a young man who found hope in a hopeless world. Without a doubt, God had blessed this young man. There was only one problem. He still carried baggage from his old life. Hidden sin was tearing his life apart, but he still had no group of godly friends with whom to be honest about his struggles.

I will never forget the day I received the phone call. Rick, the young carpenter full of vitality, was weeping like a baby on the other end of the line. He pleaded with me to meet with him. Without hesitation, I drove across town to get together with him and his pastor. He confessed that he had fallen back into sniffing rubber cement and glue. We prayed together and talked things out. I convinced him that God loved him and forgave him. But I knew one more thing was necessary. He would need a network of friends to hold him accountable. At the end of the meeting, he said, "I feel much better. I feel great." I sternly warned him that his well-being depended on building a strong group of people to help him through the tough times of temptation.

Weeks passed, and I did not hear from him. When I called his pastor, he said that Rick hadn't been in church for two weeks. Apparently, he was struggling again. The weeks turned into months, and the months turned into years.

One day, Rick drove to my house. The ultra-thin drug addict I met that day was a pale comparison to the muscular young man who once traveled with our team to proclaim hope to others. He had fallen back into the old patterns of self-destruction. Without the support of godly friends, he had become entrenched once again in a life of substance abuse and delinquency.

A group of trusted friends can help us avoid wandering off course. When they turn us from the error of our way, they save us from death and cover a multitude of sins. If you feel that your life has drifted from the direction you know you should be taking, perhaps it's time to reevaluate the course you're on and the friends you have chosen.

2. Without Godly Friends, We Fall into Unhealthy Relationships

The second consequence of not having a group of godly friends is that we often tend to fall in with people who end up doing us harm. It's a tragedy when good people allow their lives to be destroyed by unhealthy friendships. Instead of encouraging one another in a godly way, these friends spur each other on toward a life of self-destruction. Scripture tells us:

> The lips of an adulteress drip honey,
>   and her speech is smoother than oil;
> but in the end she is bitter as gall,
>   sharp as a double-edged sword.
> Her feet go down to death;
>   her steps lead straight to the grave.
> She gives no thought to the way of life;
>   her paths are crooked, but she knows it not.
>   (Proverbs 5:3–6)

I've had friends who intended to live godly lives, but because they associated with the wrong crowd, they exposed themselves to a world of substance abuse. To this day, they have not been able to break free from the grips of alcoholism. Whenever we choose to hang out with people whose standards are not healthy, we pay a significant price. Remember this important truth: you cannot help but become like the people you spend the most time with.

⚬⚬⚬

Ron suddenly dropped to the floor. His breathing was shallow, and within a minute he broke out in a cold sweat. He felt as if someone were sitting on his chest. After forty-five minutes of lying alone in his office that Saturday afternoon, he slowly stood to his feet and sluggishly walked to his car. He checked himself into the hospital, where doctors ran a series of tests.

After twelve hours, the doctors felt confident that he had not had a heart attack. But they gave him a stern warning. "Ron, if you don't knock off the cigarettes, you won't be around to warn your grandkids of the dangers of smoking."

Two days later, Bill, a member of Ron's accountability group, asked him how he was feeling. He replied, "The doctors didn't think I had a heart attack, but they warned me to. . . ." Then he stuttered, "Uh . . . they warned me to stop smoking."

"What?" Bill exclaimed. "Did you say, 'Stop smoking'?"

Ron lowered his head and nodded.

"When did you start smoking again?" Bill asked.

"About a year ago," Ron replied.

"How did it happen?" Bill asked.

Ron explained that after a long meeting on a business trip, he and a few of his coworkers hit the bar and opened up a pack of cigarettes. He never thought that one drag would ruin his fifteen-year smokeless streak. That is, in fact, what happened. Each night, after their business meetings concluded, everyone headed to the bar and relieved their stress with a bit of liquid relaxation and a few smokes. By the time his two-week assignment was finished, Ron was back up to smoking a pack a day. He never had a drinking problem, but his smoking was enough to shorten his life by thirty years.

Feeling a sense of brotherly responsibility, Bill asked the question that none of his coworkers dared to ask. "So what's your plan to kick the habit?"

"I plan on cutting down one cigarette per day," Ron said.

Then Bill put one hand on Ron's shoulder, looked him in the eyes and said, "Your plan isn't good enough!"

Ron looked shocked.

Bill continued, "Instead, write a letter to your children that explains that you love cigarettes more than you love them. When you die, I'll give it to them. As a matter of fact, I want you to write the words, 'Daddy is dead, because I loved the affects of nicotine more than I loved your embrace.'"

The look on Ron's face said it all. He was offended and horrified. He said, "But Bill, that's not true."

Bill replied, "Oh yes it is! Your kids are going to ask me, 'Why is Daddy gone?' And I really don't want to tell them the truth. I'd rather you tell them. So go ahead, and write the letter, and you have my word that I will give it to your wife and kids at your funeral."

Those were harsh words. But sometimes people need ice water thrown in their faces to help them discover the truth. Fortunately, Ron got the picture. He had an aha moment as a result of his interaction with a member of his accountability group. Since that time, he has managed to refrain from the temptation of smoking.

The people who do not bring out the best in us can resurrect destructive patterns that we thought were once dead. The wrong crowd will inevitably tear us down, encourage us to do immoral things, and lead us into temptation. Instead, we need friends who pull us upward and not downward, friends who encourage us in healthy ways.

The friends you surround yourself with will either encourage you to live a godly life or distract you from living one. That is why the Bible says:

Do not be yoked together with unbelievers. For what do righteousness and wickedness have in common? Or what fellowship can light have with darkness? What harmony is there between Christ and Belial? What does a believer have in common with an unbeliever? What agreement is there between the temple of God and idols? For we are the temple of the living God. As God has said: "I will live with them and walk among them, and I will be their God, and they will be my people."
"Therefore come out from them and be separate,"
    says the Lord.
"Touch no unclean thing,
    and I will receive you."
"I will be a Father to you,
    and you will be my sons and daughters,
    says the Lord Almighty."
                (2 Corinthians 6:14–18)

Do you ever feel that your friends tear you down instead of lift you up? Perhaps it's time to evaluate the people you call friends.

3. Without Godly Friends, We Make Decisions We Eventually Regret

When no one is around to guide us, we sometimes make decisions that we later regret. That's why it is imperative to allow others to help us stay on the right course. "He who walks with the wise grows wise, but a companion of fools suffers harm," the Bible tells us (Prov. 13:20). These wise friends encourage us to make decisions that are in line with the appropriate direction for our lives. If we lack the influence of godly people, often the decisions we make will lead to results that are not in our best interest.

⌘

I traveled with my wife and a team of students to a foreign country and stayed at the Bible school in the capital city. The tropical climate was overwhelming. Between the heat and humidity, we had to drink an enormous amount of water each day to stay hydrated. After a week of classes, one of our professors asked the ten students if any one of us wanted to preach in a local church. I enthusiastically raised my hand.

After he dismissed the class, I walked to the front and asked him, "How many people attend the church?"

He said, "About 140."

"Where is the church located?" I asked.

"On the outskirts of town," he replied.

"Is there a special activity going on that night?" I asked.

He shook his head.

"How should I prepare for this message?"

His reply reflected the frustration of a parent who had been asked too many questions. "Why don't you trust God?" he asked.

I smiled and walked away.

That Wednesday night, ten of us packed into a minivan with a four-cylinder engine. We headed to a town called Linda Vista, which means "beautiful view." Where I come from, only the wealthy have a *linda vista*. Two miles before reaching our destination, we started to climb a 10 percent grade. The minivan didn't climb any faster than the pedestrians walking home from the bus stop. I thought we might have to get out and push. After several minutes, we finally arrived at the church. Indeed, it was Linda Vista, but I didn't see much wealth in the marginalized community.

When we got out of the van we heard people in the church already clapping with the music even though it was ten minutes prior to the commencement of the service. We walked through the front door and saw that the sanctuary was packed to capacity. Seats were reserved for our group. There was only one thing that didn't seem right. Besides the ten college students, a handful of adults, and our professor (who had told me to trust God in my preparation for the church service), we were the only ones in that crowd over the age of ten.

For a moment, I thought I was in the wrong place. I quickly stepped outside to look at the door. Sure enough, on it was the word *Capilla*, which means "chapel." I walked down the center aisle, looking to my right and left. I saw that the kids' feet barely touched the ground. I felt like the Jolly Green Giant. Apparently, the pastor thought that because we were a team of young people, we would have a great presentation for the children of his church.

One boy caught my attention. He was about eight years old and wore a red windbreaker and jeans. The serious look on his face was accentuated by his military style crew cut. As I started speaking, his big brown eyes seemed to stare right through me. He had a hopeless expression. When everyone was laughing, he was lifeless. When the crowd shouted "Amen!" he said nothing. He just stared straight ahead.

When I concluded the message, I dismissed the crowd and walked over to the boy. He evaded me and quickly moved down the aisle. As he headed for the exit, I asked the pastor if he could tell me about the young man.

"Yes," he said. "His mother was a prostitute. She had no friends and no family. She became pregnant, and after his birth, she abandoned him on the streets and moved away. He moved from one orphanage to another. Lately he has been staying with a family who has an extra room. Regrettably, his mother made poor choices that will haunt her the rest of her life."

I walked to the back of the church, sat down on the steps leading to the sidewalk, and watched that eight-year-old disappear into the darkness of an impoverished town. I was convinced that his life was not a mistake. His mother's biggest mistake wasn't getting pregnant or walking the streets as a prostitute. It was abandoning her son. Perhaps family and friends would have talked some sense into her. Maybe she would have made the same choice regardless. One thing is certain. If she had been surrounded by family or friends, they might have cared for that young child.

No matter what we face, God can provide us His real power to help us get by. One of the greatest resources for strength is the energy that others provide when we feel alone. When you feel that you cannot continue, surround yourself with people who genuinely care about you. It will have a powerful and positive effect on your efforts to move forward. Remember, God is on your side and He demonstrates that many times through the love that others pour into your life!

ENERGIZED BY OTHERS

Recently I had a conversation with a young woman who told me that she had a paralyzing eating disorder. Each night, she obsessed about all the food she wanted to devour. With tears in her eyes, she said, "No one understands." Her pain was deep and overwhelming. Just because she felt that way, however, didn't mean that what she felt was the truth.

Many times when we feel lonely we get the idea that no one in the world can understand how we feel. Feeling alone is devastating, and it drains our energy.

When we surround ourselves with positive, uplifting people who truly want the best for us, we can't help but excel. They energize us. They lift us up. They carry us through the times when we lose our strength. Godly friends live by this admonition: "Do not let any unwholesome talk come out of your mouths, but only what is helpful for building others up according to

212

their needs, that it may benefit those who listen" (Eph. 4:29).

Moses was one of the greatest leaders of all time. On one particular day, Exodus 17 tells us, he was furious. The constant complaining and the threats on his life had become more than he could handle. He cried out to the Lord, "What am I to do with these people? They are ready to drag me out in the middle of a field and stone me." It wasn't the first time God heard Moses' frustration, and it wouldn't be the last.

As the nation of Israel, numbering approximately three million people, came to a place near Rephidim, they set up camp and looked for water. But there was none to be found. "We are dying of thirst out here in the desert," they cried. "Did you bring us out of Egypt just to watch us die? Don't you care about our livestock and our children? Give us something to drink now!"

Moses replied, "Why are you fighting against me? The Lord is the one who is leading us. He brought us to this place. Take it up with Him!"

When Moses expressed his frustrations to the Lord, God gave him an answer. "Grab your staff and take some of the elders and go down the road. When you come to a large rock, I'll be waiting for you there. Then strike the rock with your staff, and water will come out." Moses did what the Lord told him to do.

When the elders saw the water gushing out of the rock, they knew that God was with them.

Suddenly the Amalekites attacked the Israelites, and Moses sent a young man named Joshua to defend them. As Joshua fought against the enemies of Israel, Moses went to the top of the hill overlooking the battle. He took Aaron and Hur with him. As he stood up, holding his hands in the air, Joshua fought fiercely against the Amalekites.

With time, Moses grew tired. When he could no longer keep his hands in the air, the Amalekites began to overtake the Israelites. Then, as he regained his strength, he lifted them up and the Israelites gained the upper hand. It seemed as though there was no way to gain victory. Moses was growing tired, and he needed a solution. Finally, Aaron and Hur found a large stone and placed it under Moses so that he could sit down. Then Aaron stood on one side and Hur on the other. Each one held one of Moses' hands in the air until Joshua had defeated the entire Amalekite army. By sunset, the battle was over.

In these two stories, Moses surrounded himself with people who helped him accomplish his objectives. The elders were able to back up what Moses said about where the water came from. If anyone questioned his authority or integrity, the elders served to protect his reputation and shield him from individuals who complained. Hur and Aaron provided the necessary encouragement and energy for Moses to affect the outcome of the battle. Moses couldn't do it alone. He was not a one-man show. He needed help, and his trusted group of friends provided it.

We also need people to hold up our hands when we have no strength. When life seems overwhelming, godly friends can help us get through it. With people around us who want the best for our lives, we can find the energy to do what is right.

HONESTY VS. EMBARRASSMENT

While it is important to be surrounded by people who energize us, it does us little good if we are not completely transparent with them. As the following story illustrates, our level of honesty can determine whether or not we head into a disaster or experience victory.

As our plane pulled away from the gate at Newark International Airport, the captain fired up the engines—first the left, then the right. We came to the end of the taxiway and waited to be cleared for takeoff. I looked out the window and noticed something I had never seen on any flight.

Just under the left engine, liquid was dripping onto

the concrete. It looked like raindrops, but there wasn't a cloud in the sky. The liquid was spraying off the engine at about a cup a minute.

Well, I thought. *I can sit here and say nothing. But if the engine blows up in mid flight, I'll most likely regret my silence. Is my pride worth the lives of everyone on the flight?*

The flight attendant was sitting at the bulkhead of the aircraft, facing the rest of the passengers. We sat about four rows from her. Without further hesitation, I called her over and showed her what I saw. She said, "I'll inform the captain."

The first officer came quickly, nodded, and stared at his watch and out the window for nearly a minute. Finally, he said, "Forty-two drops per minute. I'll tell the captain."

Several minutes passed, then the captain said, "Ladies and gentlemen, one of the passengers noticed some liquid dripping out of the left engine. The first officer has confirmed it. We're returning to the terminal to have maintenance take a look at it, because we believe in safety first."

The other flight attendant looked at me, gave me a thumbs up, and mouthed, "Thank you!" We returned to the gate, where maintenance looked over the engine to make sure everything was in working order.

After we had taken off, I got up to use the restroom. As I passed the flight attendant, she said, "I am so glad you called our attention to the problem. Imagine if something worse had happened. We would like to say thank you. Would you and your family like some chocolate sundaes from first class?"

When they brought the desserts back to us, the family lit up. My girls turned to me and said, "Hey, Dad, can you find anything else wrong with the plane?" Not only did telling the truth help to promote our safety, it paid a nice dividend.

Many times we avoid telling the truth to others because we fear rejection or embarrassment. These fears prevent us from being open and honest, but that hurts only us. Transparency with God and others keeps us on the right path. I believe that God puts His hand on our shoulder and says, "It's okay. Everything will work out just fine. Trust in Me and be honest." When we are sincere and honest, the truth has a powerful way of liberating us. As Scripture says, "Then you will know the truth, and the truth will set you free" (John 8:32).

I once heard a speaker say, "I've discovered that I am either in the middle of a trial, coming out of one, or going into one. The tragedy is the people in my life aren't helping!" While I was convinced about trials and how often we face them, I couldn't help but think, *Just what kind of people do you hang out with?*

⌒◈◌⌒

Bartimaeus, who had lost his sight, found his usual spot along the road and begged for money. That day, Jesus and His disciples passed by with a huge entourage of people. Bartimaeus asked those who were standing next to him what all the commotion was. "Jesus, the great healer, is passing by," they replied.

When he heard that the Master had come to his town, his heart filled with hope for a miracle, a life-changing opportunity. To Bartimaeus, Jesus represented the ultimate power to change. So he raised his voice above the noise of the crowd and said, "Jesus, Son of David, have mercy on me!"

In Mark 10:48 we see something interesting at this point in the story. It says, "Many rebuked him and told him to be quiet." Bartimaeus would hear nothing of it. He raised his voice all the more. "Son of David, have mercy on me!"

That's when Jesus stopped and said, "Bring him to me." Then Mark writes, "So they called to the blind man, 'Cheer up! On your feet! He's calling you'" (v. 49).

Jesus asked him, "What do you want me to do for you?" The blind man said, "Rabbi, I want to see."

"Go," said Jesus, "your faith has healed you" (vv. 51–52).

Interestingly, when Bartimaeus was a lonely beggar, the people rebuked him. When Jesus called him, he became a star, and everyone sang his praises. None of his friends were supportive until they saw that he was moving up the social ladder. God wants us to have better friends than this.

PEOPLE WHO LIFT US UP INSTEAD OF TEAR US DOWN

There is no substitute for a friend who lifts us up instead of tears us down. Godly friends are edifying. They carry us when we can no longer make it on our own.

∽◇∾

Year after year, the man's only source of mobility was the friends and family members who carried him from place to place on a stretcher. He had no hope for change. He had no hope for recovery. He depended exclusively on the mercy of others, that is, until that one encounter that changed his life forever.

Rumors were circulating about a man called Jesus who had the reputation of healing the sick. That day, He was teaching in a house a few blocks away.

Four men who loved their paralyzed friend decided to take him to see the healer. They felt that if he met Jesus face-to-face, something extraordinary would happen. About an hour before the meeting, they picked up their friend, placed him on a mat, and carried him a significant distance.

When they arrived at the house where Jesus was, they discovered hundreds of people trying to get inside. Although there was no way the four men could get through the crowd with their friend, they were not about to turn back. They had come too far to give up. One friend said to another, "I can't believe this. After walking all that distance, we won't be able to see Jesus." Then another one said, "Hey, I've got an idea. Why don't we take him up on the roof and lower him through the tiles?"

"Are you crazy?" said the other two. "How are we going to lift him to the edge of the roof? Besides, what will the owner think when we start tearing a hole in his roof?" The other friend replied, "God has opened this door of opportunity. Let's give it a try." The four friends finally agreed. Two of them climbed up on the roof while the other two lifted the man as high as they could. They pulled him to the edge and held him there until the other two friends could climb up as well.

The four carefully walked across the roof looking for the right spot. One of them asked, "Where do you think the healer is standing?"

"He's probably over there," said another, pointing to the center of the house.

Just twelve feet under them, Jesus was teaching the large crowd. The audience was made up of Pharisees and teachers of the law who had come from every village in Galilee and the surrounding areas. Some were genuinely interested in hearing what He had to say. Others were looking for an opportunity to trap Him. In spite of the pockets of opposition, God was with Him to heal those who needed help.

On top of the roof, two friends fervently removed tiles to create the opportunity for an encounter, while the other two held their paralyzed friend in place. The hole they created was large enough to lower him on his mat. Their calculation was accurate. Carefully, they managed to place their friend at the Master's feet.

When Jesus looked up and saw their extraordinary efforts, He was amazed. Their faith impressed Him. Jesus knew that in order for the paralyzed man to receive his miracle, he would need to remove something that stood in the way. Of all the problems the man had, his physical impairment was the least of his concerns. The most significant barrier he faced was sin. Christ, filled with compassion, reached out and said, "Friend, your sins are forgiven."

Immediately, the teachers of the law became furious, although they didn't say anything to him. They said to themselves, "Who does this guy think he is? No man can forgive sins except for God. This is blasphemy!"

Perhaps it was the sour look on their faces or the fact that they refused to look Him in the eye. Either way, Jesus sensed the opposition. He knew they didn't like what they just heard. "Why do you have such a hard time with this?" He asked. "Why does forgiving someone bother you so much? Tell me, which is easier to say, 'Your sins are forgiven,' or to say 'Get up and walk'?" (Luke 5:23).

In their minds, one was blasphemous. The other was miraculous. There are never any guarantees for a miracle, and they knew it. They couldn't conceive of a scenario where a human being could have the authority to forgive sins. So they had no answer.

Christ turned this into a teachable moment. If you can heal someone who is paralyzed, He told them, you must be divine. If you are divine, you must tell the truth. So if you can heal someone, you can, therefore, forgive his sins. Filled with self-assurance and confidence, Jesus raised His voice and said, "I am the Son of Man, and God has given me authority on earth to forgive sins." Then He turned His focus from the teachers of the law to the man lying on the mat and held out His hand with the palm up. "I tell you, get up, take your mat and go home."

Suddenly, nerves that never functioned before began sending signals through the man's spinal cord into his cerebral cortex. For the first time, he felt a tingling sensation that was indescribable. Immediately he stood up and to the dismay of the teachers of the law, picked up his mat, and headed for the door. As he walked through the crowd, he glanced back at Jesus and smiled. Then he looked over at the Pharisees and smirked. After a pause, he raised his hands, turned toward the door, and screamed, "Hallelujah!" The crowd erupted in praise.

The man's four friends peeked through the hole high above everyone's head. The look on their faces said it all. Their tears of joy confirmed what they felt in their hearts at the beginning of the day. They jumped to their feet and quickly made their way to the side of the building where they climbed down to greet their friend. This time, they didn't need to bend over to embrace him.

Those inside the house were amazed and gave

praise to God. They were filled with awe and said, "We have seen remarkable things today" (story paraphrased from Luke 5:17–26 and Mark 2:1–12).

The paralyzed man had no chance for healing that day had it not been for the loving friendship of four men. They faithfully carried him so that he could meet Jesus face-to-face and receive a miracle. Their names are not recorded in the Bible or in any history book, but they were a beautiful example of a trusted group of friends who looked out for the best interests of their friend. They went all out for him, and when it seemed as though reaching their goal was impossible, they explored all the options until they found a way to succeed.

Do you have friends who love you like that? Would your closest friends do whatever is necessary to see that you are healthy and safe? Are you surrounded by people who want the best for you? I pray that you are. You deserve great friends. God wants you to be surrounded with loving, caring people. He wants to see you build a group of godly friends.

CREATING AN ACCOUNTABILITY GROUP

If you're serious about living a life of freedom and power, put into practice the following keys for creating a group of people who will lift you up instead of tear you down.

1. Choose People Who Will Be Committed to You

Chances are, God has already placed wonderful people in your life who can help you overcome the things that hold you back. Ask the Lord to help you identify those individuals who will keep you moving in the right direction. Your spouse, parents, friends, and people at church can help guide you toward your goals. (If you are working on your marriage or family relationships and do not have the confidence to ask them to be a part of your group, focus instead on friends and church members.)

In a healthy marriage, *your spouse* is the first person to consider. Marriage is a union in which a husband and wife vow to take care of one another. For better or worse, in sickness and in health, a couple is committed to encouraging each other to walk in the right direction. You can trust your spouse to help you overcome the issues you face. You can share things with your spouse that you cannot share with anyone else. God designed marriage to be a safe haven. "For this reason a man will leave his father and mother and be united to his wife, and they will become one flesh" (Gen. 2:24).

In a healthy family, *parents* and other *family members* are the second group to consider. I'm sure you are wondering, *Didn't you say that we pick up destructive patterns from past generations?* Yes, but this book is not about blaming our parents. Do not discount your parents and family as viable assets to help you in the course of life. Most parents are wonderful gifts from God who want the best for their children. We honor them by embracing the good they hand down to us. "'Honor your father and mother'—which is the first commandment with a promise—'that it may go well with you and that you may enjoy long life on the earth'" (Eph. 6:2–3).

Friends are the third group to consider. In addition to your spouse and family, perhaps you have friends who are willing to speak openly and honestly with you. Often they can better serve you in this capacity because they tend not to be tangled in sibling rivalries or have a history of competition with you. Furthermore, with friends you have an established history of confidence. You already know if you can trust them, and decent friends usually do not treat their friends with disrespect.

Your church is an excellent resource for people who are both godly and willing to help. Discipleship is a core value in many churches. Not only do they have strong curriculums for accountability, but they also have people who can help guide you in the process of putting together a group that is right for you. Especially if you are married, select people who are of the same gender as you. Any time you share details about the temptations you face, you become vulnerable. Having a group of the same gender greatly reduces the possibility of developing an inappropriate relationship with someone in your group.

Once you have an idea of the people you want to ask to be in your accountability group, begin thinking about them in light of the tone, commitment, honesty, and spiritual level you want in your group. Having these elements clear in your mind will help you choose the folks who will help you create a healthy and godly group.

2. Tell Your Accountability Group That You're a Quitter

Before you begin meeting with your accountability group, tell them you want to be a quitter. That is, you want to quit smoking, drinking, cussing, overspending, losing your temper, eating junk food, watching too much television, or whatever you want to stop doing. Give them permission to ask you about your progress on a regular basis. Just knowing that you will have to face their questions will be a strong deterrent.

3. Make Sure Your Group Is Positive and Uplifting

Every time you meet with your group, there should be an atmosphere that promotes your personal growth. Insist that the tone be positive and uplifting. Make sure that your group of trusted friends builds you up rather than tears you down. "Everyone should be quick to listen, slow to speak and slow to become angry" (James 1:19).

Regardless of your victories or defeats, you ought to feel loved, encouraged, and accepted by your team of trusted friends. When you feel you cannot go forward, their strength and support will carry you through. "Carry each other's burdens, and in this way you will fulfill the law of Christ" (Gal. 6:2).

4. Meet Regularly

Meeting on a regular basis is one of the most important keys to a healthy accountability group. There will be times when meeting on a regular basis is difficult or doesn't seem important. But consistency is necessary for your accountability group to be effective. So commit to meet regularly and be transparent about your victories, defeats, and struggles. "Let us hold unswervingly to the hope we profess, for he who promised is faithful. And let us consider how we may spur one another on toward love and good deeds. Let us not give up meeting together, as some are in the habit of doing, but let us encourage one another—and all the more as you see the Day approaching" (Heb. 10:23–25).

5. Be Transparent Yet Confidential

Everyone involved in your accountability group should feel free to share his or her heart without fear of being refuted, judged, or lectured. Everything that is shared should be kept in confidence, because some people may share something that is personal and may not want it repeated. Everyone should try to refrain from saying things behind someone else's back. "A perverse man stirs up dissension, and a gossip separates close friends" (Prov. 16:28).

6. Make Prayer an Essential Part of Your Experience

Take the opportunity during your time together to pray. Of all the things we can do in a support group, prayer is the most important. Something happens when others lift us up in prayer. Bondages are broken. Vices lose their power over us. Hope fills our hearts, and healing comes to us in a wonderful way. Praying for one another is one way we experience God's love and concern. "Therefore confess your sins to each other and pray for each other so that you may be healed. The prayer of a righteous man is powerful and effective" (James 5:16).

HOW I FOUND A GROUP THAT WAS RIGHT FOR ME

"Hi, my name is Jane, and I'm an ACA."

"Hello, Jane," the group replied.

Those were the first words I ever heard in a small group. I will never forget walking into the Twelve-Step meeting for Adult Children of Alcoholics (ACA) and sitting down in the semicircle. I was twenty-two years old and didn't know anyone else in the room. To make matters more interesting, I was the only male and the youngest member. The middle-aged women told horrific accounts of lives filled with physical abuse, drug addiction, alcoholism, pain, and tragedy. Two of them were struggling to make their third and fourth marriages work. Others were recovering from twenty years of substance abuse. At my age, I hadn't yet developed a good poker face. With each testimony, my jaw dropped further and further. I genuinely felt sorry for them, but I had a hard time feeling that I belonged in that group.

When it was my turn to share, I said, "You know, I feel pretty good about my life. I mean, yeah, my mom struggled with alcoholism but nothing like what I've heard here tonight."

I'm quite sure they didn't appreciate my comment. At the end of the meeting, only one woman said, "Well, we hope to see you next week."

Although I didn't return to that group, I still had the desire to release the troubling things I was carrying. Two weeks later, I walked into a local church. It had a small-group curriculum designed for people who wanted to break the patterns of generational dysfunction. The group was comprised of both men and women with a few who were my age. This time, I decided to stay.

Each week, we shared the struggles we endured and our hopes for a better future. We operated under an agreement of confidentiality, which prohibited any of us from repeating outside the walls of our meeting place the information we shared. This created an atmosphere of security, trust, and openness. Being able to share in this capacity and meeting on a regular basis helped solidify God's healing process in us.

After six months, I was a different man. The time I spent in my small group brought tremendous healing in my heart. I am so convinced of its effectiveness that I decided to dedicate a whole chapter in this book to encourage you to make meeting with a supportive small group a priority in your process for change.

God offers you real power at a time when you most need it. A close network of trusted friends in whom you can confide can keep you from wandering off course, falling into temptation, and making decisions you'll later regret. As long as your group is open, uplifting, committed, honest, and willing to pray, you will experience tremendous transformation. Your greatest days will come quickly.

Before we close this chapter, I would like to leave you with a final thought. My mom had many struggles and difficulties in her life. She traveled through the darkness of depression during the early 1990s. She survived the death of a spouse, and as a widow, she lived alone for many years. I can honestly say that she has fully embraced the six steps suggested in this book, especially this one. She has done an excellent job of establishing relationships in church that have aided her in her spiritual growth. At a time when it could have been easy to run and hide or shut everyone out, she decided to seek God's help. She started reading the Bible and praying. She attended a local church. She established healthy relationships with people of like faith.

If my family can overcome the destructive patterns that are passed from one generation to the next, if we can experience the liberating power of Christ, and if we can overcome the chains of bondage, then just imagine what God can do in your life. Imagine what He can do in your family. Imagine what He can do in your marriage or with your children. Imagine the possibilities and potential that God has laid out before you. You are the apple of His eye, and He is rooting for you.

⁓✖⁓

Once again, we will end this chapter with a short prayer. By now, you understand how important prayer is as we reach out to God to be transformed. Together we will ask God for direction so that our lives will be surrounded by the right people who can help us with this final step.

Lord, I thank You that You love me so much. I realize how fortunate I truly am. You care deeply about my life, and You want me to stay on track. It is not Your will that I drift off course. So I ask You to help me find the right

*friends and people I can trust. May a group of
trusted associates help me keep my eyes on
You. Whenever I get blown off course, may
they give me the necessary counsel so that I do
not fall back into patterns of self-destruction. I
need Your guidance. I ask You to help me see
with Your eyes and hear with Your ears. I ask
You to give me the mind of Christ and the wisdom of God in all things. I commit my life to
You, and I ask this in Christ's precious name.
Amen.*

Unleash Real Power in Your Life!

——————— ❦ ———————

RECENTLY A FRIEND SENT ME an e-mail mentioning an interesting study done about a hundred years ago. The study examined two individuals, contemporaries who lived in New York, and their family descendants. The study looked at the effects of the lives of these two men upon their children and the generations that followed.

One of the men did not believe in God and promoted a life of free sex, no rules, and no responsibilities. The second man was known for being disciplined. He became a pastor and led by strong example. He authored several books and preached to many people in his lifetime. Most importantly, he partnered with God, and the decisions he made were a direct reflection of that partnership. He married a woman who had deep spiritual convictions and a committed relationship with God.

The results of the values of these two men upon their descendants could not have been more different. The first man had 1,026 descendants, of whom three hundred were convicts, 190 were prostitutes, twenty-seven were murderers, and 509 became addicted to alcohol or drugs. Up to the 1950s, his descendants had cost the State of New York $1.2 million. By contrast, the second man had 929 descendants, of whom 430 were ministers, 314 were war veterans, seventy-five were authors, eighty-six were college professors, thirteen were university presidents, seven were congressman, three were governors, and one was a vice president of the United States.[1]

The first man rejected God. The second partnered with Him. One produced descendants who were a burden to society. The other created descendants who shaped society. One chose a life of debauchery. The other chose a life of discipline. One walked in self-destruction. The other walked in the blessings of God.

There is a lesson to be learned here about how our lives affect the generations that follow us. If we choose alcohol, drugs, materialism, debauchery, or reckless living over God's plan, we pay a heavy price and so does the next generation. If we fall into patterns of self-destruction, we are not the only ones who suffer—the generations that follow us suffer as well. A life filled with idolatry produces emotional and spiritual dysfunction that will plague the next three and four generations (Exod. 20:5).

Conversely, if we choose to walk with God, our descendants will reap a blessing. A life partnered with God leaves a rich heritage for those who follow. Following God's spiritual laws will produce blessings in your family for a thousand generations (Exod. 20:6). The central message of this book is simple: a life with God is much better than a life without Him. Because of Him, our lives are blessed. A life without Him is plagued with self-destruction, loneliness, depression, and alienation.

The second man in the study mentioned above was eighteenth-century pastor and theologian Jonathan Edwards. He made a difference with his life, as did his descendants. Edwards left behind a great heritage that continues to this day. As you reflect upon your life, what kind of heritage are you leaving? If your life was to be studied, would it be considered a blessing for the generations that follow you? What are you passing on to the next generation?

As I write this book, I sense God's overwhelming

love for you. I know that He believes in you and is willing to empower you to change the destructive things in your life. He wants you to make a quantum leap forward—He is your biggest fan! So if you're not living the life you want, acting on the six steps that we have covered in this book will help you experience the breakthrough you seek. Because these six steps are so crucial to your transformation, let's review them again.

1. DISCOVER YOUR *WHY*

Before personal transformation can occur, we must discover why we want to change. Because our desire to be different fuels the change we long for, our reasons for changing must be stronger than our excuses for not changing. If they aren't stronger, we won't be able to access God's power to reinvent ourselves.

2. CHANGE YOUR PERCEPTIONS

When the destructive patterns in our lives keep us from seeing the light of hope, we need to change our perceptions. This change begins with seeing our lives for what they truly are. And as our eyes are opened, we recognize the need for God's involvement in every part of our lives.

3. BREAK THE CYCLE OF DESTRUCTIVE BEHAVIOR

The third step in our journey toward freedom is to identify the destructive behavior patterns passed on to us by previous generations. We break their influence over us and over the generations that follow by tapping into three powerful keys—a constant transfer of leadership, learning to deal with temptation, and becoming aware of what we say, feel, and do.

4. FORM GODLY HABITS

Who we are and the choices we make are largely determined by the way we think. Godly thoughts lead to blessing. Ungodly thoughts lead us toward destruction. If we want to see God's power in our lives, we choose to transform our thinking by taking on the mind of Christ. Three powerful habits help to renew our minds and ultimately shape our destinies: listening to biblical teaching, fellowshiping with one another, and prayer.

5. CHOOSE TO FORGIVE

Bitterness is like a poison we drink hoping to inflict pain on those we hold in contempt. But it only winds up hurting us. If we do not manage to forgive those who have offended us, we inevitably face devastating consequences. The bitterness that takes root in us does not disappear over time. Instead, it only worsens until we make a decision to let it go. The Lord's prescription is simple: forgiveness is a decision, not an emotion. Forgiveness is also an ongoing process. When feelings of betrayal and hurt come back to the surface, we remind ourselves to continually choose to put the past in the past.

6. OVERCOME WITH THE HELP OF OTHERS

Surrounding ourselves with godly people is one of the most important steps in our transformation. Without that accountability to others, we stand in great danger of drifting off course. The eyes, ears, and senses of people of like faith give us direction. We need their objectivity, especially in times of trouble and transition.

A FINAL WORD

Finally I want to say to you, *stay the course*. Although the wind will blow and turbulence will make the air around you unstable, God will give you the guidance you need. He will uphold you with His righteous right hand (Isa. 41:10).

Expect delays in the process of reinventing yourself. Changing your life is not done overnight. Many of the patterns of destruction in which we find ourselves take years to form. And it will take time to move beyond them. In many ways, it's like going on a diet. If it takes us twenty years to gain fifty pounds, we shouldn't expect to lose that weight in a week. When transformation seems slow, remember that God is in your corner, and you will win the good fight.

God desires to turn your disasters into victories. He wants to see your children walk in His blessings. He wants to break the things that hold you back through a partnership you form with Him. He wants your life to be blessed. He wants you to experience new life.

The only true solution for breaking the chains of oppression, addiction, and dysfunction is the power that Christ gives us through a daily relationship with Him. That is precisely what I hope you experience. That is my prayer for your life.

In every chapter I have included a prayer that you can use as you talk with God. Now I want to close this book and our time together by praying for you. Imagine that I place my hand on your shoulder as I pray the following for you:

Lord, I lift up my friend who holds this book in his or her hands. Fill every gap in this wonderful life You've created. May You provide for every need, touch every area, and set this life free from everything that holds it back. I know the great potential You see in this beautiful life. I believe that the greatest days for my friend are fast approaching. So I ask You to open wonderful doors and pour your blessings into the life of my friend. Move this life beyond the destructive patterns he or she is currently facing. Bring about a new day, where negative self-talk dissipates and the attacks of the enemy begin to recede.

Initiate Your habits and Your way of thinking so that my friend can experience Your power and strength in every area of life. Give my friend the strength to live a life of forgiveness and freedom from all bitterness. Surround my friend with people who will keep him or her accountable and on the right course with You. I ask that the past, present, and future be a legacy of Your strength and testimony and that You will bless this person and his or her family for a thousand generations! I ask this in Your precious and holy name, Christ Jesus. Amen.

May God richly bless you in every area of your life!

Questions for Reflection and Group Discussion

—— ⟨⟩ ——

INTRODUCTION: DO YOU NEED THE POWER TO REINVENT YOURSELF?

There has never been the slightest doubt in my mind that the God who started this great work in you would keep at it and bring it to a flourishing finish on the very day Christ Jesus appears. (Philippians 1:6 *The Message*)

Questions for Personal Reflection
1. In what area of your life do you need to experience a breakthrough?
2. What are some of your greatest personal frustrations?
3. If you could snap your fingers and make three

specific things happen immediately, what would you want to happen?

4. What is the one thing about your life that you've always wanted to change?

5. What keeps you awake at night?

6. Are you who you want to be? If not, what adjustments do you feel you need to make?

Questions for Group Discussion

1. In what ways do you feel stuck?

2. In your opinion, does God want you to live a victorious life? If so, what does that life look like?

3. What is necessary in order for God to have the freedom to begin transforming your life?

Applications

1. Every day, remind yourself that God loves you and that you are someone He fearfully and wonderfully created. He can transform your life as long as you are willing.

2. The Lord wants you to give you freedom, joy, peace, and the desires of your heart. As Jesus said, "The thief comes only to steal and kill and destroy; I have come that they may have life, and have it to the full" (John 10:10).

CHAPTER 1: DISCOVER YOUR *WHY*

And you, my son Solomon, acknowledge the God of your father, and serve him with wholehearted devotion and with a willing mind, for the LORD searches every heart and understands every motive behind the thoughts. If you seek him, he will be found by you; but if you forsake him, he will reject you forever. (1 Chronicles 28:9)

Questions for Personal Reflection

1. Think of a time when you changed something about your life. What motivated you? What empowered you to complete the task?
2. What is your *why* (reason) for change? Are you motivated by fear, goals, disgust, or a desire for a healthier life?
3. Are there issues in your life you've never been able to resolve? If so, what are they? In your opinion, why have you never been able to resolve them?
4. What is the *Yes, but...* (excuse) that has kept you in the same place?
5. If the Lord asked you, "What do you want me to do for you?" what would be your response? Why?

Questions for Group Discussion

1. What would you like to see happen in your life as a result of going through the material in this book?
2. Can you become who God wants you to be *and* who you want to be?
3. What is the biggest reason that you haven't moved forward?

Applications

1. Tell yourself each morning that with God, *all things are possible* (Matt. 19:26). As you endeavor to break the destructive patterns in your life, remember that God will empower you to do so.
2. Write out a *why* (reason for change) that is right for you. Think about how that will motivate you to partner with God to reinvent yourself.

CHAPTER 2: CHANGE YOUR PERCEPTIONS

The god of this age has blinded the minds of unbelievers, so that they cannot see the light of the gospel of the glory of Christ, who is the image of God. (2 Corinthians 4:4)

Questions for Personal Reflection

1. What relationships, conflicts, tragedies, difficulties, or challenges have formed the way you perceive the world?
2. What erroneous ways of thinking need to be changed in order for you to stop surviving and start living?
3. In what ways do you feel that Satan has clouded your perception?
4. Is there a destructive pattern that you want to break? Is it a pattern that has affected previous generations in your family?
5. Did you ever say to yourself: "When I grow up, I'm going to be different from my parents. I will never treat others the way I am treated!" In what way did you want to be different? Are you different?

Questions for Group Discussion

1. In what ways can an unhealthy perception keep you from living the life you want to live?
2. What was the impact of Moses' encounter with God on the mountain? How did it change his perception?
3. How can a relationship with God reflect the true condition of your character, disposition, and attitude? How is this helpful in your quest to reinvent yourself? Why is this so important? What role does the Bible play in helping to remove a contorted perception?

Applications

1. Read John 8:32 and ask God to help you discover the truth about what holds you back. Begin reading the book of John on a daily basis to discover truth. Give God permission to help you get past the destructive patterns in your life.
2. Make a point to remember that regardless of your background, God wants you to experience a powerful transformation. According to Him, you are the apple of His eye (Zech. 2:8).

CHAPTER 3: BREAK THE CYCLE OF DESTRUCTIVE BEHAVIOR

You shall not bow down to them or worship them; for I, the LORD your God, am a jealous God, punishing the children for the sin of the fathers to the third and fourth generation of those who hate me but showing love to a thousand [generations] of those who love me and keep my commandments. (Exodus 20:5–6)

Questions for Personal Reflection

1. What do you regularly, consistently, or habitually seek that brings gratification or a high in a time of need, hurt, or anxiety?
2. Do you have any idols that keep you from healthy, godly living?
3. If Christ came to help people who are stuck in destructive patterns, in what specific ways can He help you experience freedom?
4. What area of your life do you feel is the most difficult to transfer leadership over to God?
5. What are some of your greatest temptations?
6. As you endeavor to break the cycle, what practical steps can you take to become aware of what you say, feel, and do?

Questions for Group Discussion

1. Do you notice a correlation between when you feel anxious and when you engage in destructive behavior?

2. In what ways does breaking the first two commandments affect the generations that follow us? What are some examples of idols in our society today?

3. If previous generations have developed patterns of destruction, are we condemned to follow in their footsteps? If not, what is the solution that God offers us?

4. What are some practical things you've done to overcome temptation?

Applications

1. The three keys to freedom are transferring the leadership of your life over to God, learning to deal with temptation, and becoming aware of what you say, feel, and do. How can you implement these keys in your life?

2. When you are anxious, ask yourself: *What am I feeling right now? Do I feel hopeless, angry, hurt, resentful?* Look for a way to express your true feelings to the Lord, and ask Him for help in dealing with them. Think of 1 Peter 5:7: "Cast all your anxiety on him because he cares for you."

CHAPTER 4: FORM GODLY HABITS

Do not conform any longer to the pattern of this world, but be transformed by the renewing of your mind. Then you will be able to test and approve what God's will is—his good, pleasing and perfect will. (Romans 12:2)

Questions for Personal Reflection

1. Is it true that we can change our destinies if we change our mind-sets? If so, what do you want your destiny to look like? What sort of mind-set would you need in order to reach your desired destiny?
2. What are some of the destructive things you say to yourself time and time again? How can you combat those destructive thoughts? What are some biblical examples for healthy self-talk?
3. What practical things can you do to make every thought obedient to Christ?
4. What are some of the thoughts that God wants you to think?
5. How does prayer change our internal and external worlds? How do you feel when you connect with God in a real and meaningful conversation?

Questions for Group Discussion

1. How can we acquire the mind of Christ? Why is this so important in the process of true self-reinvention?
2. In what ways are your thoughts the greatest adversary you face?
3. How does studying the Bible, spending time in fellowship, and prayer help you to change your life? What results can you expect in your life by practicing these things?

Applications

1. Try to spend time each day reading your Bible.
2. Look for those who have similar faith, and invest time in a meaningful relationship with them.
3. Take time each day to have a meaningful conversation with the Lord.

CHAPTER 5: CHOOSE TO FORGIVE

"In your anger do not sin": Do not let the sun go down while you are still angry, and do not give the devil a foothold. (Ephesians 4:26–27)

Questions for Personal Reflection

1. Is there someone that you've been unable to forgive?
2. Has there been an incident in your life that you felt was unjust, and as a result, you've held discontent against the Lord?
3. Do you need to forgive yourself for something you've done to someone (or to yourself)?
4. In what ways can bitterness and anger become poisonous, contagious, and binding?
5. Why must forgiveness be a choice?
6. How has God displayed forgiveness toward you? In what ways have you experienced His forgiveness?
7. Is it more difficult for you to forgive people who couldn't care less that they've hurt you or to ask people whom you don't think you've hurt to forgive you? In what area is your pride the strongest?

Questions for Group Discussion

1. What happens to us when we refuse to forgive those who have offended us?
2. Does time heal everything?
3. What were the consequences for King David's family because of his initial refusal to come clean and turn from his evil desires? (See 2 Samuel 11, 12:1–22.)
4. What steps can we take to extend forgiveness to those who have hurt us?

Applications

1. Take a sheet of paper and write out the names of those who have hurt you.
   Then in an audible voice, say each name, followed by the phrase, "I forgive you." Remember the Lord's Prayer, and ask God to help you find the strength to forgive those who have offended you (Luke 11:2–4).
2. When you do not feel like forgiving those who hurt you, remember this: if someone has negatively affected your past, don't give that person the opportunity of messing up

your future. Release the person and let the offense go. "Take my yoke upon you and learn from me, for I am gentle and humble in heart, and you will find rest for your souls" (Matt. 11:29).

CHAPTER 6: OVERCOME WITH THE HELP OF OTHERS

My brothers, if one of you should wander from the truth and someone should bring him back, remember this: Whoever turns a sinner from the error of his way will save him from death and cover over a multitude of sins. (James 5: 19–20)

Questions for Personal Reflection

1. In what challenging areas of your life do you feel that godly friends would be an encouragement? How could they help you overcome the things that are holding you back?
2. Do you have a friend who tears you down instead of lifts you up? Why are you attracted to him or her?
3. What sort of person could you become, what great things could you accomplish, and what destructive patterns could you overcome if you had a trusted group of godly friends to help you in these areas?
4. Think of the six people with whom you spend the most time. Count your family as one

person. Chances are you will become like those six people. Is this desirable? Are they who you want to become?

Questions for Group Discussion

1. Why is having an accountability group comprised of people of the same gender important?
2. What does the Bible say about the kinds of friends we choose to hang out with?
3. How can we find a balance between having friends who may not share our faith and surrounding ourselves with people who encourage us in godly living?

Applications

1. Ask God to help you discover the right people to help you move forward. Remember, God answers prayer. "Don't fret or worry. Instead of worrying, pray. Let petitions and praises shape your worries into prayers, letting God know your concerns" (Phil. 4:6 *The Message*).
2. Take a sheet of paper and write out the names of people you believe will make up the right accountability group for you. Ask them if they are willing to commit to doing this for you.

Notes

—— ⌘ ——

Chapter 3: Break the Cycle of Destructive Behavior

1. Michael Windle, "Concepts and Issues in COA Research," *Alcohol Health and Research World* 21(3): 185–91. http://en.wikipedia.org/wiki/Alcoholism_in _family_systems#cite_note-WINDLE1997-9
2. Richard D. Dobbins, "Bonds and Boundaries in Your Relationship with God." http://www.drdobbins.com/ guidelines-details.asp?artid=80&catid=100

Chapter 4: Form Godly Habits

1. "NCC's 2009 Yearbook of American & Canadian Churches reports decline in Catholic, Southern Baptist membership." *News from the National*

Council of Churches (New York: Feb. 23, 2009).
http://www.ncccusa.org/news/090130yearbook1
.html

2. Hunter Baker, "Is Church Attendance Declining?" *Christianity Today* (Web-only) (Nov. 08, 2007). http://www.christianitytoday.com/ct/2007/novemberweb-only/145-42.0.html

3. Claudia Wallis, Jeanne McDowell, Alice Park, Lisa H. Towle, "Faith & Healing," *Time.com* (Jun. 24, 1996). http://www.time.com/time/magazine/article/0,9171,984737,00.html

Chapter 5: Choose to Forgive

1. William J. Cromie, "Anger can break your heart." *Harvard University Gazette* (Sept. 21, 2006). http://www.news.harvard.edu/gazette/2006/09.21/01-anger.html

2. Sandra Ray, "Stress-Related Diseases," *Livestrong .com* (Jul. 16, 2009). http://www.livestrong.com/article/5960-stressrelated-diseases/

3. S. I. McMillen and David E. Stern, *None of These Diseases* (Grand Rapids, Mich.: Fleming H. Revell, a division of Baker Publishing Group, 1963, 1984), pp. 220–21. Used by permission.

Chapter 6: Overcome with the Help of Others

1. Retrieved from http://en.wikipedia.org/wiki/Korean _Air_Lines_Flight_007; http://conservapedia.com/ Korean_Airlines_Flight_007; http://aviation-safety .net/database/record.php?id=19830901-0

Conclusion: Unleash Real Power in Your Life!

1. "Jukes and Edwards: Significant Statistics of Two American Families," *New York Times* (July 22, 1900).

About the Author

―――――――――― ⌦ ――――――――――

JASON FRENN comes from what he humorously calls a "crazy family." While growing up in a nontraditional home where divorce, alcoholism, and family discord were the norm, he realized he couldn't break the dysfunction on his own. After a Hispanic family invited him to attend church in 1981, he began to reach out to God for help and found the strength in Christ to overcome the destructive patterns that had plagued his family for years. In 1991, he left his corporate position as a highly successful sales representative and began serving in full-time ministry. After attaining his BA in history/political science and MA in church leadership from Vanguard University, Jason and his wife moved to Costa Rica as missionaries with the Assemblies of God. Since that time, he has traveled the world as a missionary-evangelist and conference speaker. Over the years, he has held more than fifty evangelistic citywide outreaches in Latin America and the United States and has spoken to more than three million people, with two hundred thousand making first-time decisions to follow Christ.

Jason is a dynamic speaker and author who uses stirring personal testimonies and biblical principles to inspire audiences all over the world. In addition to the citywide outreaches he holds, he is a highly sought conference speaker for churches, nonprofit organizations, and business audiences. Jason is the founder of Taking It to the Nations and Power to Change International. He hosts a daily live radio program on the Radio Nueva Vida network, with a listening audience of 475,000 people. He is a frequent guest speaker on the *Hour of Power* broadcast from the Crystal Cathedral in Garden Grove, CA. For more information, you can visit his website: www.jasonfrenn.com.